GDP-BASED REPRESENTATION

Jordan David Weisinger, M.S., M.A., M.B.A

Contents

ACKNOWLEDGMENTS

This book is an abbreviated version of other books by Jordan David Weisinger titled "GDP-based Representation" (2018) and "The Fountain; Nation Building with Econometric Representation" (2018). All material in this book was resourced from the original book.

1. "Provisional Democracy describes provisional (emergency) governments during wars of succession or secession.

2. "Public Policy-based Protests: Resistance Strategies for Mayors, Governors, and Legislators" describes strategic nonviolent protest strategies like tax embargoes, default, shutdowns, and economic sanctions.

3. "Insurrection: Essays on Institutional Protests and Regime Change" describes indicators of growing authoritarian parties and public policy to reform back to democracy.

4. "Income-based Representation describes econometric representation based on income, with strong anti-discriminatory properties.

5. "Asset-based Representation describes econometric representation based on home ownership, with strong anti-discriminatory properties.

6. "Tax-based Representation describes econometric representation based on tax liabilities, with modest anti-discriminatory properties.

JORDAN DAVID WEISINGER

FORWORD

The most important property of econometric representation is its ability to extend the life of democracy by emphasizing the representation of wealthier districts and increasing the adjusted per capita income of voting residents. Higher per capita incomes are associated with states prolonging their status as a democracy. This could be a critical component of nation building exercises after occupation. If an occupying nation could better guarantee success after installing democratic entitlements in the host nation, it could justify the large amount of labor and capital spent on the effort. Anything that makes it more likely the occupied nation will achieve high quality democratic status should be considered a viable option or strategy when nation-building.

Current international treaties forbid nations or states from acquiring territory from other states using coercion or violence. However, there is no guarantee these treaties or conditions will remain enforced. The world is changing, and we are moving towards an environment where the principle economic power will be a despotic and formerly communist regime. Treaties agreed to in the 1940s may not be relevant for much longer. Prior to the development of econometric representation, nations rarely occupied other nation's with the intent on including them within a democratic union. There was too much risk. In high quality democracies, each person is afforded exactly one vote, and the inclusion of a new state could destabilize national presidential elections or legislative elections. Econometric representation changes this relationship.

The second most important property of Econometric representation is based on GDP. It permits one state to incorporate another state that gains proportional representation in the long term but has reduced representation in the first few years of the new union. States that lose wars often have decimated economies with low GDP. When GDP is used as the one of the determinants of political representation, it ensures that the occupying nation has an initial advantage in GDP and representation. However, after the new states economy is rebuilt, it will have a more equal GDP and gain representational parity with the other states in the union. This is the promise of econometric representation. The new state will have a decade or two to inculcate and acclimate to the new culture of democracy before they have a reciprocal relationship. During this incubation period, the state will benefit from an imbalance of tax subsidies and investment revenues. As the new state develops a stronger economy, it gains more and more representation, eventually gaining parity with the other states in the union.

This hypothesis has yet to be tested. The independent variable is GDP, and the dependent variable is political representation. However, there are two important intervening variables. The first and most important intervening variable is the rate of federal tax subsidy provided to less developed states in a political union. The premise is federal tax subsidies will improve a low GDP state's rate of GDP growth and thus accelerate the rate of normalization in representation. The next most important intervening variable is the quality of economic reforms passed on regional level and federal level. Fiscal policy and labor laws can have a dramatic impact on GDP growth rates between states. The expected tendency or direction of the relationship is positive; the GDP of the developing nation will increase at a faster rate than that of the developed nation as thus eventually achieve a more proportional form of representation. The faster the GDP growth rate is the greater the representation gained.

This book uses a comparison of means (roughly equated to the interval measurements of GDP/population) across two or more states/nations over time to look at representational changes in demographics and econometrics. However, this book does not offer a comparison of means for GDP/population across multiple developing nations. Developing nations might have a competitive relationship with different GDP growth rates producing much bigger changes in net representation. An interaction relationship exists. States that receive more federal tax subsidies should acquire faster rates of GDP growth regardless of developmental stage. More importantly, a less developed nation may have faster GDP growth rates, but this may be offset by the GDP advantage in the more developed nation. A nation with a smaller economy and faster GDP growth may never reach parity with a nation with a slower growth rate but a much larger economy. The last effect to be measured is the difference in population growth between the more developed nation and the less developed nation. Growth in demographic representation may be faster than growth in econometric representation

The interaction relationship suggests mixed outcomes; different states will have different outcomes based on GDP growth and population growth, especially when the intervening variable of federal subsidies and economic reforms are present. Both the null hypothesis and alternative hypothesis have strategic value when used in a mixed representation system combining both demographics and econometrics. It is possible that developing states acquire adequate GDP growth to acquire proportional representation using demographic representation as normative standard. However, contrary to the stated hypothesis, Econometric Representation often concentrates majority political power in the developed nation providing a buffer against significant changes in demographic representation. Thus, econometric representation will be more often a strategy for developed nations to retain majority political control when incorporating less developed states with faster population growth rates.

Larger wealthier states will have several incentives to expand their territorial boundaries and their electorate. The evidence suggests that developed economies can incorporate smaller and poorer states into their political unions without significant long-term risk in transferring political majorities. Imposing democracy on formerly despotic nations may be improved if they are incorporated into larger more established democracies who make long term commitments to economic stimulus through federal subsidies and improved security by a permanent presence. This could promote an environment of democratic imperialism that will offset the increased risk from climate change, wealth inequality, and the rise in economic power of despotic nations like China.

Most political systems are imposed when movements form around unsubstantiated ideologies like economic opportunity or equality. Most of the contemporary democracies were founded on the twin virtues of hope and faith. It must inspire confidence without evidence. This book plays on those tendencies. It attempts to provide a reasonable alternative to conventional demographic based democracy. None of these purported political systems currently exists. The lack of concrete examples makes rigorous testing of the hypothesis impossible. Claims are made but the actual GDP data and demographic data to support the conclusions are missing. However, with a little imagination and confidence the evidence can be conjured up and examples of econometric representation will thrive in a more competitive environment for democracy.

One of the biggest concerns for a democratic nation is employing GDP-based representational coefficients for expanding the territorial boundaries while improving the quality of representation and rights for satellite states. The only means for one state or nation to guarantee the civil liberties and rights of assumed or acquired states, is to codify protections within a Bill of Rights with amendments specifically designed to ensure the same quality of representation is distributed to all persons within the union, with the necessary checks and balances to defend those claims and natural rights.

Many nations provide their citizens inalienable rights codified within a constitution elevated above other laws, intended to protect their society and political process from duress, misinformation, or surveillance and the inability to organize resistance to administrations intending to limit tehri civil, economic, personal, and natural rights. With just six primary rights, the electorate of every member state or citizens of the political union is guaranteed several pathways to protect their own rights and those rights of the sovereign states, elevated to an even greater importance when the government was created with representational coefficients intended to assume new territories for mutual support and profit. These nations must protect themselves from the behaviors they become experts in, with an emphasis on extending the same rights to assumed territories after Constitutionally stipulated performance measures and deadlines for abbreviated rights.

On the Freedom of speech, governments will not limit the rights of free speech of private individuals, unless during a war or emergency with clearly defined parameters for length and cause, declared by the legislature and reauthorized every legislative session. The rights of the individual are superior to the rights of corporate persons or firms, with companies in the business of social media and news having the responsibility of doing no harm, or as little harm as possible through misinformation. Immunity for private firms is never authorized, unless they meet the nonpartisan media criteria for news, with references and sources, and at least a modest attempt to provide an alternative or opposite viewpoint within the same release or article (*plausible, not just possible, with references and sources as well*). private non news social media sites and aggregators may defend their freedoms of speech in the courts with other private individuals or firms, subject to the court jurisdictions their users are found or were deemed reasonable by the courts.

On the Freedom of assembly, individuals have an innate right to gather, assemble and organize, where governments, regulators, and law enforcement have superior to inferior claims for interventions, in reverse order of size, effectiveness, and proximity of jurisdiction to the protesting or organizing group, with the federal government having least authority to limit gatherings and local governments the most. The government with the most authority to regulate assembly is the government most proximate to the protest location where the residents have the greatest control over the electoral outcomes. All statutory or emergency constraints on groups of individuals must be based on cause, with safety, distance, and access prioritized as mitigating factors for limitation.

Gatherings must be peaceful, with law enforcement authorized to break up riotous or disordered and disruptive gatherings, but the public has a natural license to protest without permission, when the numbers exceed a threshold set by each jurisdiction as a percentage of overall population, despite economic disruptions for a stipulated period. The freedom of assembly also gives workers the right to join unions for representation or other nonprofit organizations intended for collective bargaining, as a check to firm or establishment power in the economies.

The affirmative right to assembly assert the natural rights of individuals to form new democratic governments within current jurisdictions by voting, as long as it is peaceable, satisfies thresholds for minimum standards for representational equity, does not attempt to disenfranchise another demographic group or class within the same sovereign jurisdiction, and is reversible by future democratic voting. Protecting the right to reorganize political territories through voting and due process invalidates most claims of secession through violence, duress, or due process for as long as the citizens continue to have regular access to honest and accurate elections within all sovereign jurisdictions.

On the Freedom from undue surveillance, searches, and seizures without explicit warrants, stipulating clear limitations on the persons, places, times, and length of surveillance and searches. All personal property seized during the arrest or search must be returned in the condition it was received within a reasonable amount of time, if it is determined the properties were not directly related to the charge, if the items are not currently prohibited under law, and if the individual was not convicted of the charge. Person property used in the act of a criminal behavior can be auctioned to the public to recover the costs of conviction and incarceration, only after the first conviction for criminal acts warranting the seizure, with all recoveries not subject to future appeals results.

There is a prohibition on secret warrants from within the court system, but exclusions are available when oversight is provided by the sovereign member states or another branch of government. All warrants must have a public component, whether it be from the public within a Grand Jury, or from other elected officials (and their surrogates) from sovereign member states. No warrant may be authorized within a single tier of government, without the consent and participation of the public, or their elected officers empaneled in a similar check or system for oversight. The oversight must be self-selecting, with limited terms, and rotating members with diversity for each court region.

An exclusion exists for public authorities collecting scrubbed data from private and public firms, collecting income, demographic, or other sensitive data, which is batched and returns to private and public use as a fee-based utility (the identifiable date must be scrubbed prior to release to the data utility). The data utility can sell the de-identified data to universities, and for-profit and nonprofit organizations, with fees to recover costs on a sliding scale based on nonprofit status and proximity to the originating jurisdiction, understanding firms and research will benefit the residents living within the state or firms operating within the state most, improving social research and generating more jobs and higher paying jobs for residents.

On the Freedom to arms, the natural right for individuals and states to bear arms and organize itself into militias is prioritized, but individual's rights are inferior to the states, limited by reasonable timeframes and exclusions established by the states and the federal government. Adult individuals are represented by their municipal governments with policing power, county representation with sheriff policing power, and state electoral power over state policing agencies, manufacturing a reasonable and sufficient superstructure for an individual's rights to arms. Member states are sovereign powers giving them an innate authority to form and fund their own state militias, navies, and air guards, but they must be guaranteed equal access to federal funding and quality in munitions and durable weapon systems.

The federal branches have a requirement to maintain half of the standing enlisted for each branch in a state equivalent for the army, navy, and air force, with units and weapon system integrated within the federal branches. The priority for deployment is prioritized for the state first, with the federal government subordinated, but subject to checks and authorities by the legislatures of the member states and federal tier. Voluntary enlistment is variable, requiring a moving trajectory with the enlisted requirement permitted to be satisfied by a per capita calculation within 10% during peacetime and 20% during times of declared war (*or any reasonable threshold*).

The extension of a superior right from an individual in active and reserve status subordinates the right for an individual's rights to bear arms conditional on a choice of not serving or being excluded from serving. All individual rights can be limited, but the parameters must be defined and proportional to the risk, with recertification required based on new evaluations.

On the Freedom of Self-governance, every sovereign jurisdiction must guarantee for its citizens and residents a democratic-republic form of government, satisfying the minimum quality standards for demographic-based representation, or declared representational coefficient within the sovereign jurisdiction, by testing each institution for independently, but emphasizing the averaged result between legislative institutions. Every sovereign jurisdiction will make every effort to ensure honest and accurate elections, elevating access as a priority above honesty and accuracy, with criminal and civil sanctions applied retroactively and in between elections, understanding tradeoffs between access and honesty can be measured and weighed for accuracy. Every sovereign jurisdiction has the responsibility to ensure identification costs, transportation costs and time, and income costs are not barriers for registration or participation in elections.

Each executive must be elected by majority votes within the institution or jurisdictions they represent and lead, with no interventions skewing the results through a non-representative mechanism, such as an electoral college, or vote by states or legislative seats, not proportional to the population or chosen representational coefficient. If an executive is elected within an institution such as a parliament, the seats of the chamber must be certified as passing the quality tests first. The only way for an executive to be elected by an institution with lower per capita representation, if the executive is paired with another executive from a more representative chamber, in a superior position with more authority or oversight than the other executive.

A bicameral legislature may include different representational coefficients, but the combination of both must satisfy a minimum standard for both, measured by its proximity to a demographic representational coefficient. The combined per-capita representation for the legislative complex (bicameral or other) must be within one standard deviation or 10-20%. Every time a census is conducted, or new member states are added to the union, state, or nation, the per capita representation test is required to affirm the quality of democratic representation is conserved. With a per capita representational test with an ideal outcome of 700,000 and a 150% aperture for acceptable ratios, opportunities for new representational coefficients like GDP, tax liabilities, income, or other demographic bases or modifiers. If a demographic chamber has a per-capita ratio of 700,000 voters per each representative and an arbitrary chamber averages 1 Senator for every 3,300,000 voters across all member- states, the combined representational ratio is 2,000,000. If the ideal representational ratio is 700,000, the 2,000,0000 combined ratio would fail a test at the ideal ratio and a ratio increased to 150% of ideal, or 1,050,000.

Individual districts or jurisdictions are one test, state representation is a second test, with the combined ratio of all chambers the third test. Every district, state, and institution must pass the quality test every census or when new members are admitted. When districts fail, the ratio can be changed by statute to fit the ideal or allowable model. When the states fail a test, a change must be made to admit a second state by dividing states or combining them, as a condition of ratifying the newer member-state. If an institution fails a combined test, after adjusting the districts, and member states, the institutions can use statutes to change the coefficient used in one or both chambers with a supermajority. The process repeats until every district, state, and institution passes the per capita representation test.

The quality control checks apply to court systems, with circuits and districts tested for per capita thresholds. Demand for court systems should be proportional to population or GDP making it a reasonable demand for per capita tests. When Judges are appointed, they are appointed only to the lowest district or circuit, with the judges electing themselves to appeals courts and supreme courts in staggard years, for discrete terms, decoupled from electoral outcomes by the appointing authority. Any change in judicial majorities and courts are delayed until they have their next elections, with results changed by the executives appointments during that time.

When nations design their institutions with representational coefficients with ability to onboard new territories, outside of the normal democratic process, the Constitution governing the citizens and sovereign jurisdictions within the original nation must have clear terms for expansion enumerated within the constitution, declaring timelines for normalization of all travel, employment, trade, and representation between the new sovereign jurisdictions, with a due process for the new territory to separate itself from the larger union peaceably, through democratic process over a times series with at least three votes over three election cycles, with one change in executive office. The result of those elections and votes are valid and permanent for all parties.

More robust constitutions will cover other aspects of civil society, economy, and government. They are no less important but are more often shaped by the current culture and expectations of both the public and political class. Most of the enumerated rights in the original U.S. The Constitution deals with resident interactions with the court systems, with access to voting the second most common type of right. A New constitution should pivot to some environmental concerns like media and education curriculum, to better guarantee more accurate information is available to the public, with self-regulating professionally licensed persons determining the process and curriculums used, free of government interventions or the bias of the current political class. Constitutions will need to provide an amendment process so the structure of the government, its institutions, and the architecture behind civil society and economy are adaptable to future unknown conditions.

On equal and equitable access and standing in courts of law and before government agencies, it is unconstitutional for one party to coerce or entice another party to deny themselves access to a government agency or court for an indefinite amount of time through contracts or agreements, including arbitration boards and other intervening institutions. All parameters and valuations of agreements seeking exemption may be reviewed by the courts for adjustments in compensations and limits, every year for equity to both the individual and community. Equitable access to the courts and legal system also pertains to hiring and paying for legal defense or representation in front of a court or government agency. Lawyering and court fees must be allocated equitably to preserve a resident person's access to unbiased courts and legal system.

The officers of courts systems within the sovereign jurisdiction can be appointed by another branch of government, but only to the unfilled positions at the lowest level of the courts. Each court system will require their judges to elect other eligible judges within the jurisdiction to the more specialized and higher courts, such as appeals and supreme courts, with those offices constrained by terms term limits, and staggered in timing to ensure a single legislative or executive election won't be the only determinant in judicial majorities in their own hierarchies. The judges will be responsible for creating their own code of ethics and professional standards, enforcing the laws with disciplinary boards, but the legislature of the sovereign jurisdiction is authorized to regulate behaviors and eligibility through professional licensing boards and criminal codes.

On the Right to self-determination, the rights to vote are extended to all persons upon the age of maturity, regardless of class, gender, sex, ethnicity, race, or belief, regardless of location or custody. Candidates for office in any sovereign jurisdiction may not be excluded on any property or characteristic of race, ethnicity, gender, sex, or belief, but term limits and mandatory retirements may be applied to elected offices based on age. Institutions may base eligibility on class, identity, or capacity but they must still pass per capita quality control tests. When states and nations are permitted to create barriers to registering to vote or accessing ballots, the current political incumbents can select their electorate before the voters can select the candidates and elected officials. Any exclusions or limitations to the right to vote and access to voting could be exploited to oppress a group of people, by class, race/ethnicity, gender, sex, or belief.

All persons born within the sovereign jurisdictions are provided citizenship, without question. All territories of the nation will be given the opportunity to hold an internal vote to ratify statehood, after every new census, with automatic consent provided by the national legislature and current member-states. Both measures are intended to blunt the fear of demographic change by immigration, with the expansion of statehood a legal and mutually equitable way to alter electorates, while ensuring territories are not a pathway to imperialism or colonialism, outside of the expansion of member-states.

On the Separations of political parties and states, all primaries for sovereign jurisdictions must be conducted as open primaries with ranked choice voting, with the states regulating minimum thresholds for support to be listed on the primary ballot. The constitution may eliminate political parties as a competitive threat to the states and citizens. Political parties are private organizations with an agenda of preserving their own access to power, pursuing the parties interests and elevating them above the sovereign jurisdictions interests and their constituents interests. A ranked choice primary system with a natural right to access the ballots and elections is the best guarantor of free and fair elections within all sovereign jurisdictions.

The sovereign states must provide public campaign finance to all candidates for office within sovereign jurisdictions. State public campaign regulations introduce more competition into the overall elections system, producing a mechanism useful in regulating the candidates, incumbents, and providing quality control tests for representatives and elected officers sent to the federal jurisdictions. By passing priority to the states, it breaks up any monopoly a national political party may earn in a private campaign finance system and prevents the incumbent political class from protecting themselves by establishing barriers for other candidates or parties.

If a state permits private campaign finance systems, it must be held inferior to the public campaign systems by evaluating the total circulating cash flows in campaigns, and establish other conditions, such as public stock status, for eligibility to make donations, using fiscal policy to limit the gross amount and redistributing the difference back to state public campaign system, or authorizing those governments without sovereign status to participate in equivalent political behaviors. The states will compete through a private campaign system, with donations exported from one jurisdiction to another, opening the door for the federal jurisdiction to regulate interstate donation limits by households, private firms, and governments, with firms and governments treated equally under the laws.

On the Separation of church and state, religious organizations receive tax exempt status for as long as they remain politically inert by not making any political contributions to candidates or PACs, making speeches referencing direct candidates or parties, and voucher or subsidy for school. Tax exempt status is determined by location or incorporation or accounting cash flows, with serious infractions of political activity or speech resulting in suspension of the tax-exempt status, determined by the taxing authorities in jurisdictions. All schools sponsored by religious organizations, acting as surrogates for public schools must conform to the same curriculum standards as public schools or other private schools, or they lose eligibility for private school vouchers and the sponsoring churches loses tax exempt status, unless the religious group falls below the statutory threshold for establishment religious groups. Religious groups have an exemption if they don't exceed two thresholds on maximum participation, one is a maximum population in the state the group resides in, and the second threshold is for the overall population. When a religious group falls below the upper bounds of the threshold, it is exempt from any curriculum standards for their proprietary or charter schools. The threshold is set by statute and can be modified the year after each census.

On the Freedom from misinformation, media companies in the business of news, must be honest and accurate. Media platforms only have immunity for providing News, if the information presented is generally accurate and passes through traditional quality controls for News in various media. Social media providers are required to accept liability for what is posted by subscribers and users, subject to current civil case laws and courts, forcing them to police and supervise the content made available to their users. To be considered News and use a News label for any logos advertising and branding, it must apply the journalistic quality to 70-80% of its programming (and associated revenues). No immunity is provided for firms or organizations or media not conforming to this standard, for every quarter this test fails.

Self-regulatory boards for all sovereign jurisdictions must establish professional standards, procedures, and disciplinary boards for licensed journalists, and certified News providers. Journalists do not need to be sponsored by firms or employers, with the education and tests widely available and low costs. Only credentialed journalists can sit on the boards from each state, and each board can elect their own members to the national board (representative of population). All media, including digital or social, and other providers can only acquire immunity if the posts labeled as News are produced by employees under the supervision and direction of licensed, credentialed, and certified journalists. Governments may not intervene in any aspect, other than providing the mandatory funding and enforcing the civil fines, penalties, and sanctions through the court system, when firms fall to perform under the standards

On the freedom to information, every sovereign jurisdiction is compelled to provide free public education to all residents, with an equivalent quality and funding between municipalities. The sovereign jurisdictions all have the authority to determine the curriculums within their education systems, but through boards composed of licensed educators elected to the state boards from municipal or county boards formed from elected educators from publicly managed educational institutions. The self-regulating boards determine guidelines for state schools, and design the regulatory regimes for discipline, grading, appeals processes, and other aspects of publicly funded and managed schools and education systems for all enrolled residents. The administrations and staff of the schools are responsible for implementing the policies and enforcing the regulations. The sovereign jurisdictions will ensure all residents and citizens are not discriminated against for any reason related to class, ethnicity, race, or age (below mandatory retirement).

On the natural right to body autonomy, it extends to reproductive rights and control over medical procedures impacting their bodies, a right to rehabilitation for incarcerated persons, protections for workers from slavery, indentured servitudes, and deregulated labor markets. On the natural right to body autonomy, every resident has the right to rehabilitation proportional to the difference in average longevity at the current age, considering sentence estimates with behavior evaluations, with a second check for rehabilitation as a productive internal member when life sentences or longer sentences are issued. To ensure compliance, no prisons or jails may be operated for profit and all prison labor must be paid the statutory minimum wage for all applicable sovereign jurisdictions. On those natural rights not incorporated by enumerated rights and amendments, with a tendency for autonomy for those persons under custodial care, like parents, prisoners, or those institutionalized, covering medical, labor, and other domains.

A critical right is the claim to the natural rights not enumerated within the constitution and amendments, which is purposefully ambiguous to permit the courts a tendency to rule for residents and citizens over non-natural persons and sovereign jurisdictions, taking into consideration public good and unacknowledged or unidentified future conditions as a limitation to those natural rights. The natural rights to life, liberty, nutrition, and other aspects of survival are claimed by individuals as the basis for social-welfare and other fundamental aspects of democratic government and a well-regulated market economy. A limitation on corporate personhood claim to rights as non-natural persons is permitted, all public companies seeking to exercise the freedoms and rights given to natural persons, on an equal basis, not inferior or limited basis, must grant labor unions or employees seats on their corporate boards. Public companies not elevating their employees to a threshold determined by statute will lose the rights and protections extended to firms.

On Federalism and sovereignty, the new nation is incorporated with sovereign member states working within a sovereign federal tier, providing powers for the federal jurisdiction and rights for each state and the citizens' rights. If at incorporation, no sovereign member states existed, the county, provinces, or applicable territory will be elevated to sovereign state within the federal system for as long as the federal system of sovereign jurisdiction exists, and the legal and final boundaries can be enforced. The sovereign states have all applicable enumerated and natural rights afforded to the residents and citizens within the union. A Supremacy clause will elevate federal laws to a superior position over state laws but limits the federal government to only those domains of law enumerated within the powers of the legislature, with the sovereign states given authority to pass laws on all other domains unless the Constitution is amended to include other domains.

On Amending the constitution, two tracts must be available for amendments, one for the federal government, checked by consent by the states, one for the states without oversight by the federal government, with only the product from institutions satisfying the per capita thresholds for quality control remaining valid. The states must have their own pathway to amendments, in cases where the federal government has carved out incumbent powers for itself and elevated its interests above those of the states and citizens. At the time of incorporation, the member-states and their federal representatives can determine the ratification process and all voting thresholds, if it satisfies the per capita quality control for each sovereign jurisdiction for the initial vote and the oversight vote, when applicable.

JORDAN DAVID WEISINGER

1 ECONOMETRIC REPRESENTATION

It is human nature to reorganize our environment in a manner that produces more security and more order. One of our greatest tools in this endeavor is the state. States allow us to marshal our productivity and harness our resources. They provide a common defense against those external persons that would exploit us or harm us. They also provide for law and order to protect us against those internal persons who would exploit or marginalize us. However, for all their self-evident benefits, we continue to succumb to ancient tribalism and partisan belief systems when it comes to immigration and expansionism. This is especially true, when democratic representation is intimately connected to demographics.

Econometric representation is a major innovation in disentangling representation from the arbitrary representation of senates. The Senate is a regressive form of representation that overtly contradicts the tenants of self-governance and majority rule (*i.e., consensus*). Senates distribute an equal number of representatives to each state regardless of their populations or other attributes. Therefore, arbitrary representation is essentially an inverse of demographic based representation. The two tend to cancel each other out resulting in increased stagnation and obstruction. Bicameral legislatures rely on cooperation between two chambers to pass economic regulations and fully fund the government. Decoupling representation from majority consent introduces political instability and the possibility of catastrophe or conflict.

The use of Gross Domestic Product (GDP) as a representational coefficient is a less extreme option than the arbitrary representation of a senate. Political unions predicated on a combination of Gross Domestic Product and demographics will help insulate representation from demographic changes. This is a significant improvement for political unions which helps dispel fears of coercion when integrating two large populations with different cultures or economic prospects. Gross Domestic Product is a simple measurement that occurs over a district or state jurisdiction. It is an aggregate measurement of economic activity for a large and diverse community. This helps distance it from a single ethnicity, tribe, or religion in more open societies. More specifically, GDP is the total dollar value of all goods and services produced over a specific period [1].

GDP isn't an accurate measure of individual wealth, and it is only weakly correlated to population in nations with high variance between aggregate economic activity. However, the value in using GDP for a representational coefficient is that it is standardized and denominated in a common currency. Standardization is the key property to consider. A nation can reasonably calculate its current GDP in relation to another nation's GDP. It can examine its trajectory for growth in comparison to other countries comparison to growth. Current options are constrained by current theory, and GDP is easily translated into representational coefficients

---

[1] Gregory N. Mankiw, The Essentials of Economics (6th ed.) (Stanford: CT Cengage Learning, 2015), page 309.

for use in class-based systems of representation. All the calculations in this book use GDP as the baseline, but GDP can be easily substituted with Gross National Income (GNP). GNP is "the total income earned by the nation's permanent residents"[2]. The difference and their uses can be debated.

There are two primary methods to allocate GDP based representation among participating nations and states. The first method is the straight method, and it assigns a number of representatives to each state in accord with the proportional value of GDP compared to other states in the Union. The second method is called a median partition and is more complicated. The districts or states are ordered according to GDP and split into two equal parts by the median GDP value. Both methods conform to the standards of universal suffrage but the median partition preserves majority rule. They offer excellent alternatives for demographic representation when nation building or forming political unions. Each has its own advantages depending on the circumstances.

Straight GDP based representation allows a nation to incorporate new states without dramatically changing the disposition of their own legislative chambers in the near term. The assuming nation can expand its population base for consumption or conscription. It can gain access to natural resources and geo-spatial advantages. The recently incorporated state gains some potent benefits. In the near term, the state gains access to tax subsidies and investment revenues for faster economic growth. More importantly, it also receives martial support to protect voting rights and ensure the new republican form of government has an opportunity to root in culture and

---

[2] Gregory N. Mankiw, The Essentials of Economics (6th ed.) (Stanford: CT Cengage Learning, 2015), page 313.

expectations. In the long run, GDP based representation will provide an opportunity for the state to acquire full representation in a stable democracy with a mature economy. All participating states will benefit from the new relationship, albeit at different times during the re-organization. This is the promise made. Sacrifice now for the future benefit of improved security and increased equity.

Straight GDP based representation will result in a concentration of representatives in wealthier states. This isn't representative of population but many institutions in contemporary democracies aren't either. Senates are notorious for over-representing rural states and smaller states. Those states are often poorer with fewer residents. This allows exploitative economic policies to propagate through the nation despite the majority objecting to them. It allows corporations to deregulate labor markets and obstruct environmental laws. It reinforces counterproductive policies like austerity measures and regressive taxes. Arbitrary representation is often a deficiency, but it should conform to contemporary standards for representation in systems aspiring for Universal Suffrage.

The imbalance in representation within econometric systems is purposefully engineered; it allows the more successful partners to project their financial management expertise and culture the other states within the Union. The single market and single currency zone will promote investment and trade within the less developed economy and eventually the currency exchange rates will equilibrate. More importantly, the lower GDP states should receive a larger proportion of federal tax subsidies promoting faster GDP growth with the economic stimulus and engineering. When parity in per capita GDP is earned, the state will receive proportional representation and acquire equal status with the other states. This is the promise of economic integration. This is the promise of citizenship and union.

Econometric representation should improve outcomes in nation building when the wealthier cities and regions earn proportionally more representation in the fledgling democracy. The ability to maintain democracy is dependent on the nation's ability to acquire economic security for its citizens. "The expected life of democracy in a country with per capita income under $1,000 is about eight years. Between $1,001 and $2,000, an average democracy can expect to endure 18 years. But above $6,000, democracy lasts forever"[3]. Econometric Representation emphasizes the political will of the regions with higher per capita incomes over those regions with lower per capita income presenting an opportunity to capture outcomes usually associated with higher economic output.

For example, a per capita income of $900 might include regions with per capita incomes of $1200 and $600. If the regions with per capita incomes of $1200 earned more proportional representation, it could effectively prolong the life of the democracy from 8 years to 18 years. The additional 10 years may give a fledgling democracy an opportunity to pass economic reforms raising the average per capita income passed the $1000 threshold and extend state longevity. To test this hypothesis, a nation must first accept the use of GDP as a representational coefficient in their legislature. This requires trust and trust is hard earned.

---

[3] Adam Przeworski, Minimalist Conception of Democracy: A Defense." In Democracy's Value edited by Shapiro, I. and Hacker-Cordon, C. (Cambridge: Cambridge University), page 16.

Administrations should examine econometric representation as an option for nation building after occupations. Econometric representation can produce a per capita income that is much higher when adjusted in proportion of net representation in the union. The first step in the calculation is taking the number of representatives from the demographic representational coefficient and multiplying the figure by the per capita income for the state. These values are summed and divided by the total number of representatives. The modified per capita income uses a number of representatives based on a GDP based representational coefficient. The GDP for each state is tallied and divided by the pre-determined number of representatives. The GDP of each state is then divided by this number with all non-whole numbers rounded down except those less than 1. All values less than one are rounded up to one. The new number of representatives is multiplied by the per capita income. These figures are tallied and divided by the total number of representatives producing the modified per capita income.

The hypothesis that a modified per capita income will result in greater longevity will remain untested until an occupying nation or rebel group agrees to the terms of GDP-based representational coefficients in a democracy. Most democracies have a second chamber to their legislatures introducing an intervening variable in most experiments. The rational is GDP-based representational coefficient emphasizes states with higher GDP simulating a state with a higher per capita income. Each state will include an electorate that incorporates residents of all income brackets with diversity in ethnicity and religion. This helps justify the emphasis of wealthier states within the political union. These wealthier states will in turn pursue sounder economic policies that contribute to wage growth and economic stability.

Take India as another example. India had a per capita income of $1627 in 2015[4]. If GDP was used as a representational coefficient in India instead of population, the modified per capita income increases to $1929[5]. This 18.58%[6] increase in per capita GDP could be meaningful in terms of state longevity. This could effectively double the expected period for preserving democratic entitlements passed the 18 years predicted at $1627[7]. Increasing per capita to over $2000 is suddenly a short-term goal when viewed through the prism of a modified per capita income of $1929. Other nations like Iraq may have more profound outcomes. It has a current per capita income of $5695 and a GDP-based representational coefficient might easily inflate the figure above the $6000 threshold for permanent democracy[8]. This is an important strategic goal of the occupying force from 2004. If econometric representation makes success more likely than it will be viewed as a viable option during other nation building efforts.

The impact of econometric representation on democratic longevity may be more important for less developed nations. Take for example Afghanistan with a per capita GDP of $590[9] and the tentative grasp it has on

---

[4] "GDP per capita India", StatisticsTimes.com, accessed on April 2nd, 2018 at
http://statisticstimes.com/economy/gdp-capita-of-india.php

[5] "Indian states by GDP", Worldatlas.com, accessed on April 2nd, 2018 at
https://www.worldatlas.com/articles/indian-states-by-gdp.html

[6] This is an imperfect translation. It does not include the 12 nominated representatives in the lower house. The GDP-based representational coefficient produced 228 base representatives rather than the current 233 without the nominated representatives

[7] Adam Przeworski, Minimalist Conception of Democracy: A Defense." In Democracy's Value edited by Shapiro, I. and Hacker-Cordon, C. (Cambridge: Cambridge University), page 16.

[8] "Iraq: GDP per capita", Trading Economics, accessed on April 2nd, 018 from
https://tradingeconomics.com/iraq/gdp-per-capita

democracy. If the lifespan of a democracy with $590 GDP is only 8 years, then raising it passed $1000 could be a critical strategy for preserving democracy. If Afghanistan's modified per capita income could be raised above $1,000 it could extend the timeframe for achieving durable democracy from just 8 years to 18 years or more. Afghanistan is America's longest war with nearly 17 years of active combat[10]. If Afghanistan accepted the use of GDP-based representational coefficients, its legislature would emphasize the wealthier states over the poorer and more rural states providing an arc to more stability and more equitable economic reforms. These reforms can include minimum wage laws, union protections, progressive taxes and other simple reforms. Accelerated GDP growth over 17 years may have pushed its modified per capita income passed the $1,000 threshold helping suppress support for the Taliban. The higher modified per capita income could extend the life of the democracy until it acquired enough wealth to perpetuate itself indefinitely. This is the promise of GDP-based representational coefficients for nation building. However, without a controlled experiment this speculation will remain unproven.

Representational coefficients also offer more potential for peaceful integration of nations and states. The promise of one person and one vote is a powerful inducement for Union. The assimilated states will likely have less developed economies limiting their GDP based representation on the federal tier. Larger populations will have less net representation in the initial union. However, as the economy matures, the currency will gain value and

---

[9] Accessed on 4/2/2018 at https://www.worldatlas.com/finance/afghanistan/gdp.html

[10] Accessed on 4/4/2018 from http://abcnews.go.com/Politics/afghanistan-americas-longest-war/story?id=10770029

the region's GDP will grow in value along with the number of representatives apportioned to the state. It permits the assuming nation to take on a new state without necessarily disrupting its current fragile balance in leadership and political representation.

In peacetimes, these political unions will be cooperative efforts. They will be negotiated by lawyers and economists in the bureaucracy of government. The process will be metered out over years or decades with several generations participating in the process. Trade negotiations will expand into currency zones. Uninhibited travel and labor movement will follow. Eventually, the nations' will agree to share political representation and modest regulatory control. Each phase is a step towards complete integration as a single economic and political union.

History doesn't always move so slowly. In war time, these political unions will be part of expansionist designs for democratic empire. The premise of imperial democracy is a notion that is anchored in history. The Romans forged for themselves an empire that stretched across hundreds of thousands of square miles. It bestowed citizenship on the elite within the conquered cities and nations. This allowed them to pacify populations that would otherwise persist in turmoil and pursue revolt at every opportunity. Contemporary econometric systems have this capacity too.

GDP based representation distributes universal suffrage among the newly incorporated people that is nearly indistinguishable to the quality of suffrage provided to the other citizens. Net Representation is still a function of wealth, with the federal level while each eligible citizen continues to receive one full vote (one person one vote). Within the region, the citizens will continue to benefit from proportional representation on the local and state level. Legislators within the GDP based chamber will represent only a small portion of the total number of elections. Most of their representatives will be elected on a local level, producing equivalency between the voters of that city or region. The integrated nation will preserve a large part of their independence despite losing sovereignty to the larger nation with a more mature economy. Often, national elections for Presidents are based on majority rule or popular votes. This will offset the non-proportional representation found within the bicameral legislature.

One person one vote qualifies as universal suffrage even if the tenant of majority rule is violated. Majority rule is assumed to be a core component of democracy, but the earliest versions of democracy all included restricted electorates. People only assume democracy is predicated on majority rule. This is the promise of demographic chambers of representation. However, claims of majority rule can easily be disputed by the incorporation of the Senate based on arbitrary representation. All arbitrary systems of representation actively counteract or mitigate the majority rule provided by demographic chambers. In this respect, econometric representation based on GDP can be declared as high-quality democratic entitlements despite relying more on universal suffrage than majority rule.

Political Unions with non-proportional representation will rely on marketing their Constitutions and civil liberties when trying to strike a deal. A strong Constitution can fill the vacuum when a low GDP doesn't provide substantial and reciprocal upfront representation. A strong Constitution gives a new state an immediate benefit rather than a future benefit. The people will still expect economic development and a substantial improvement in GDP and representation, but the Democratic institutions protecting civil liberties from a constitution will imbue patience and discipline in the electorate. This is significantly more important, if the assume nation was previously despotic or totalitarian where citizens were routinely tortured, imprisoned, or murdered for free speech or political activism.

Civil liberties promote non-violent protest, and they have demonstrated to be nearly twice as effective as armed insurrection or riot. A stable democracy with strong civil rights agencies and other Democratic institutions will help ensure the new population inculcates into the culture of peaceful civil disobedience and faith in the due process of democracy. These virtues make it more likely that the new state adopts the culture of democracy and its positive institutions. This will improve outcomes in nation building with special emphasis on the democratization movement.

GDP based representation helps diffuse tensions from changes in the demographics of a union. This should make it possible to avoid demographic-based violence. If representation isn't completely predicated on demographics there is very little fear in losing political power to an emergent population with a growth rate larger than the current majority population. Demographic fears are an overarching concern in many democracies where nativism and populism can cause social upheaval, unrest, riots, and civil wars. Worse, it can result in direct and imminent threat to democracy and due process in the nation.

GDP representation continues to rely on personal voting, but it disrupts the direct translation of political power from population size. GDP carries some parity with demographic based systems of representation when located within the same nation, but it has a weak association with populations between nations split by mature economy or developing economy status. This makes political unions between states of different population and wealth to coordinate their political and economic activity while preserving universal suffrage. It is intended to limit the severity of demographic shifts by diffusing the magnitude of political power transferred when one demographic group loses majority status and another gain's it. If the representational coefficients were never exclusively based on population, the fear of loss is ablated by the uncertainty in representational outcomes.

The primary role of GDP based representation is to minimize the correlation of population with political power but there is no legitimate way to disentangle individual votes from political outcomes. This makes all political systems vulnerable to political instability resulting from demographic shifts. Nothing will change the fact that another demographic group acquires majority status within a state, but if that state doesn't receive a number of representatives equal to its population, the perceived risk to other demographic groups is lessened. A higher variance in representation between states undergoing demographic shifts reduces the risk of loss of political power. The loss of power is moderated by the variance between states, and this obfuscates the risk.

This sounds like an affront on the very nature of democracy, but the purpose of the senate and a bicameral process was to insulate the nation from animal spirits in the population. Arbitrary representation is an inverse to population which takes the power away from the majority demographic group. However, senates are not always effective in this respect. A senate creates the opportunity for a minority to monopolize the legislative process and completely obstruct due process and reform. Although, senates were intended to be the bulwark against nativism and populism, their design has aided it. It is often the less densely populated and poorer states, with less educated residents and more homogenous electorates, that benefit from the inverse of demographic political representation Most nativist and populist movements come from these regions creating a dangerous trend in national sentiments and public policy.

GDP based representation is intended to achieve the same goals without this increased risk from minority political party control. GDP typically favors more diverse regions with more educated residents. This implicitly checks the momentum of a populist movement. Not only are wealthier states less prone to nativist tendencies but they will have significantly more political power. States with larger metropolitan areas and more educated workforces will have more GDP and more representatives in the federal legislature. This is true in systems that utilize a straight GDP representational coefficient and those that use a median partition.

Econometric representation may make class tensions worse with the possibility of substituting wealth-based conflict. However, class-based tensions are safer and more productive than demographic based tensions. Most class-based tensions can be addressed by economic reforms and tax reforms. Institutions like Unions can reduce poverty and improve wealth equality. Most demographic attributes are fixed and permanent over a lifetime. The only solution is anti-democratic policies limiting voting rights and election. Obviously, this is a terrible response and counter-productive in every aspect.

This makes demographic shifts intrinsically more dangerous than periods of wealth inequality

Civil disobedience through peaceful protest would be successful at earning economic reforms. This is not true for demographic instability. Nothing will satisfy the growing anger in a population that fears it is being crowded out by another population. Democracy is a terrifying process as it peacefully transfers majority political power from one majority demographic group to another. It is even more terrifying when one majority group has been responsible for exploiting or oppressing the other for generations with austerity measures and deregulated labor laws. The majority demographic group would have to permanently alter the trajectory of the nation with mass incarcerations, mass murders, or anti-democratic measures like voter suppression or voter fraud. Class tensions are far easy to mitigate, with progressive taxes, minimum wage laws, and unionization rights. Class based representation increases the odds a nation will identify the issues or policies that will address the instability and then more easily pass them. Nations can't completely exclude the possibility for riots, violence, or civil war as it is often a mix of both demographic and class-based tensions, but they can reduce the frequency and magnitude with GDP based representation.

The alternative to straight GDP representation is the median partition. Median partitions are primarily class-based systems that separate above median GDP states or districts from below median GDP states or districts. Two co-equal chambers are created, with all citizens retaining one person one vote and the legitimacy of majority rule. Class based representation helps the electorate align their public policy to their interests and then facilitate bargaining and negotiation between the above median GDP class and the below median GDP class. The bicameral legislature will require each class to barter and compromise on legislation resulting in higher quality laws containing benefits for both classes.

There are three types of median partitions. A standard median partition uses a demographic representational coefficient to determine the number of representatives each state receives, but it then arranges the individual districts from highest GDP to lowest GDP and splits them in half at the median value. There are an equal number of districts in the above median GDP chamber and the below median GDP chamber. A biaxial median partition allocates states to above median GDP and below median GDP chambers with the larger more populous states concentrated in one chamber. The states are arranged by GDP from highest to lowest and split between the two chambers. The third variety is Senatorial. It continues to divide the states between the above median and below median chambers, but this version drops the demographic representational coefficient and allocates an arbitrary number of senators per state.

A median partition concentrates districts with similar median incomes into similar representational regions. Districts with lower GDP will belong within a legislative chamber with other low GDP districts. Higher GDP districts will participate in a legislative chamber with higher GDP districts. This makes it more likely that the wealthiest citizens will vote in elections with other wealthy citizens. It also makes it more likely that poorer citizens vote for candidates representing poor jurisdictions. They will form more accurate class identities within their respective chambers helping facilitate more informed debate between the above median GDP and below median GDP chambers.

Within statewide jurisdictions, the variance between incomes within the population is significantly higher. Greater variance produces less homogenous electorates and less predictable outcomes. However, a more diverse electorate has other advantages. Its lack of homogeny is built on different perspectives and economic outcomes. This should contribute to debate on policy options. More importantly, less predictable electoral outcomes keep political parties more honest and make the political system more competitive. Dividing states by median GDP will help shape the political preference of their residents and the class identity. This is a small concession, but it does make the conditions more acceptable for developing nations when they are integrating into political unions with more mature economies. They will find solace in caucusing with states of similar economic status.

The intersection of states and districts by GDP forms classes of governments. It splits the nation into "haves" and "have nots". The class division will aid in issue identity and then conflict resolution. High GDP regions will have different concerns than low GDP regions. Labor laws, federal tax policy, education, and healthcare issues may be viewed differently by the two competing classes. It also splits the nation into urban districts and rural classes. The role specialization within the chambers should allow them to negotiate more effectively. It is simply a higher form of organization for democratic representation. Class based representation will significantly improve the deliberative process by focusing on the interests of the two groups.

The median partition avoids many of the pitfalls of wealth-based representation calculated by weakly correlated or poorly defined econometric figures. Median partition often uses demographic representational coefficients reaffirming majority control over a political system. GDP is used as a means of separating the electorate by class rather than assigning political power to the wealth attribute. In a median partition, poor districts or states have just as much political representation and power as wealthy districts or states. This is not true in straight GDP representation that assigns a number of representatives based on its comparative economic activity. It is easier for persons to object to a straight GDP based system of representation based on the over representation of the wealthier communities.

2 DEMOCRATIC IMPERIALISM

Democracy inhibits imperial expansion in two major ways. When a population has access to due process and can self-regulate, they are far less interested in waging war for territorial gain. Peace is the best means to improve the economy in an efficiently regulated and adequately taxed economy. This was not true in the age of mercantilism and monarchy. In those conditions, the economy suffered under a zero percent growth rate. For a nation to expand its economy, it had to expand into other markets, most often by violence or subversion. This was not productive. Worse, monarchs were loath to extend any representational rights to the conquered cities or states. Large empires were formed with weak associations and no loyalty. The instability eventually produced a democratic revolution and the start of a new era in history. It was an improvement on the Magna Carta and resurrected the democratic policies of the Greek and Roman eras.

However, the emergence of democracy didn't end Imperialism. Imperialism continued even during periods where major reform movements towards democracy were rooted in the Americas and common in Europe. The United States maintained several possessions despite its status as the progenitor contemporary democracy. Great Britain maintained most of its territorial possessions until the end of World War II – and that accounted for nearly 25% of the world's landmass[11]. France preserved its territorial possession in Southeast Asia until roughly 20 years after the conclusion of World War II[12]. Many of the nation's still retain small islands as protectorates or territories with special rights but the movement is almost exhausted. Imperialism appears to be a dead movement. However, climate change may produce instability and opportunity to resurrect the old science of imperialism.

There is another risk. The world is watching the emergence of China as the next dominant economic superpower, and it is uncertain if the old habits of colonialism and imperialism won't creep back into the domain of acceptable behavior. The financial influence of a despotic economic superpower may imbalance the current ecology of low-quality democracies. Wealth inequality is present making them more susceptible to regime change and revolution. Economy was a powerful inducement towards democracy, when democracies commanded the majority of GDP. Now that China is emergent, the world may slip back into a period of sustained imperialism as the moral framework in the world's democracies buckles under the compromise of despotic commerce.

To counter-act these dangerous conditions, democracies may seek to expand their political boundaries through negotiated treaty or force. Each time they incorporate a new territory, they increase the population that can be enlisted into their armed forces, they improve access to natural resources, and they gain access to new economic markets for profit and government revenues. More importantly, nations   can

---

[11] Richard Halloran, "The Sad, Dark End of the British Empire", Politico.com, last modified on August 26, 2014. http://www.politico.com/magazine/story/ 2014/08/the-sad-end-of-the-british-empire-110362

[12] "Battlefield Vietnam", PBS.org, accessed on June 24th, 2017. http://www.pbs.org/battlefieldvietnam/

spread the culture of democracy and self-determination. The more people participating in democracy, the more likely it is to survive global pandemics, world wars, or economic collapses. This is especially important, in an environment seeing the rise of despotism and climate related instability. Democratic nations will need to defend themselves by scaling up their resources and eliminating threats as they are encountered. A larger number of conflicts increases the number of opportunities for democratic expansion helping to mitigate the increased environmental risks.

The core principle of self-rule in democracy is not always contradictory to expansionary policies. The most successful democratic empires all extend citizenship voting rights to conquered people. However, this expansion of the electorate is often the most dangerous consequence of imperial democracy. Incorporating a larger population into the electorate might change it. Expanding the electorate is also the momentum behind its success. Otherwise, conquered nations require too much labor and capital to continue to oppress. The act breeds contempt and suspicion in its own public and outright hatred in the occupied territory. This doesn't only drain treasuries; it also destroys labor. It demoralizes the soldiers and increasing the numbers of disabled and wounded warriors. Worse, it is a vector for antidemocratic tendencies in the population of the conquering nation. The soldiers and the public internalize the violence, and this can negatively impact their expectations, their ambitions, or their intentions.

The imperial democracies of history didn't distribute voting rights to all people equally. They didn't conform to contemporary standards of universal suffrage and equality. Restrictive electorates allow nations to expand their borders by acquiring new territory and then providing a voter entitlement to a select group within the conquered people. Distributing votes exclusively to the aristocracy will elicit support from the wealthiest citizens and help quell any dissent from the lower classes. It was the wealth and power of the landed aristocracy that allowed the assuming nations to maintain power in the newly acquired state. They would regularly put down uprisings and riots to maintain the status quo. This facilitated a quicker integration into the imperial democracy despite the fact a large majority of the public remained subjects rather than citizens.

If a democratic nation conquers another nation with the intent to expand its territory and impart voting rights to the entire population, it will quickly lose its national character. The conquered populations could easily vote in their own leaders and possibly assume control over the entire republic. A conquering nation could be dominated by a larger and more homogenous population within the assumed territory. The Conservative populations that were most inclined to imperialism were the most discouraged by expanding the electorate to include newly conquered people. For this reason, democratic empire was never pursued. In the few examples of expansion available, the conquering nation usually exhausted the host population or native population or denied them due process and voting rights in the republic.

GDP based representation accommodates these defects by establishing a variable rate of representation that increases over time. At first, the new territory may have abridged rights but after a few decades of economic reforms they should acquire more proportional representation within the empire or the union. Developing economies integrated into political unions with mature economies should get more tax support in addition from the combined benefits of pro-growth policies on the local or state level and more investment from allied states. This should improve the rate at which they assume mature market attributes with more equitable GDP distribution between the states of the new union. The assuming nation (or conquering nation) can therefore expand it borders and economy without fear of losing its mandate in the electorate, at least until the new states are inculcated into the culture and establish firm business and personal relationships within the greater population.

Predicating representation on GDP allows a host nation to incorporate another nation into its political union without excluding any persons from the electorate. Unlike the Imperial Democracies of ancient history, the new democracy need not rely on just the aristocracy. When GDP is used as an index for representation, the integrity of universal suffrage is preserved but the aggregate voting power of the new electorate is diminished. This isn't optimal from an ideological perspective, but there is no perfect solution when expanding political unions between mature economies and developing economics. The lower quality representation should conform to more situations and satisfy more conditions for political union. The greater frequency of unionization will the efficiency in the political markets even if the equity is not perfect.

The expectation is the two economies will eventually reach equilibrium and provide more proportional representation to all the citizens in the Union. Most unions already accept representational deficiencies between states. This was the original intention of the Senate in the United States. Only the idealization of a more representative system can be achieved with expansion. It is doubtful that two already incorporated states will agree to perfectly representative systems during unionization negotiations. However, the promise of nearly perfect representation creates a compact between the newly incorporated states and the host nation. Every time a new state is incorporated into the empire, or political union, it has an opportunity to acquire full citizenship status with proportional representation. It will be equal among the other states when all accept the variable representation based on Gross Domestic Product. This is the promise made.

In 1776, the original framers of United States were not too concerned with the legitimacy of a democracy based on majority rule. When the United States was first incorporated, it was an aristocratic slave state that required nearly 250 years of reforms to make it compliant with universal suffrage and the due process we now associate with contemporary democracy. Not only had they installed a Senate with nonproportional representation, but they also advocated for the Electoral college. They organized a restricted electorate that excluded the poor, women, and minorities, with only a small proportion of the total body politic retained the right to vote. Under different conditions, our revolutionary leaders might have come to alternative conclusions and made different decisions. The founding fathers were elitists and might have had affinities for a wealth-based system of representation. If the founding fathers had GDP data to draw from, they may have substituted GDP based representation for demographic representation. They may have also substituted GDP representation for Senatorial representation.

The Senate was a compromise to smaller states for accepting the House, which was predicated on demographic representation. The House provided proportional representation based on population. Thus, the more populous states would have proportionally more representation. Smaller states feared this arrangement. They thought they would be overwhelmed and dominated by the larger states. Senates operate as an inverse to demographic representation. The smaller a state is in terms of population, the greater its proportional representation in the Senate. Most contemporary democracies rely on Senatorial representation.

The Senate serves the same purpose in a political system that utilizes GDP for representational coefficients. The senate will favor the underrepresented new state by reducing the proportional representation afforded to states with higher GDP and more mature economies. Each new state can be provided with the typical number of senators thus increasing their total net representation. Senates served the same purpose by enticing poorer states into unions with wealthier states when an exclusively demographic based representation was used while still maintaining a more favorable ratio for older more established states. This is a basis for more equal representation at the onset, which isn't conditional on economic performance or currency exchange rates. The senate will be an inducement towards unionization that all new states will see as favorable.

The imbalance of representation usually found in the Senate is an upfront payment on the promise of full citizenship in the future. As the new state's economy improves with a stronger economic performance and currency exchange rate, it will rely less on the senate and more on the more proportional GDP based representation.

Arbitrary representation from the Senate is also a guarantee on continued representation despite economic performance. If GDP growth should falter in the developing economy, the new state will have already acquired representational parity with the richer states in that institution. States with excessively high GDP will receive as much representation in the Senate as states with very low GDP. The Senate splits the difference in possible outcomes, averaging out the product of population and GDP.

GDP based representation is a reasonable substitute for the Senate too. Outside of being an inducement to unionization, it is almost completely counterproductive. If one is to accept the legitimacy of demographic representation due to the innate authority of the majority population, then senatorial representation is entirely unacceptable. A nation could employ both a demographic system of representation and a GDP based system of representation. This would eliminate the arbitrary representation and substitute it with coefficients correlated with education and population density. This combination respects the implicit authority of majority rule and consensus by affording it more representational power. It is not a perfect ratio, but a meritocracy that rewards improved economic performance may outperform those nations still relying on arbitrary representation in bicameral legislatures.

If states and nations are willing to accept the high representational ratios in arbitrary systems like the Senate, they may also be willing to accept the terms for GDP representation. This is especially true in cases where a demographic chamber is also present, providing a gradient towards proportional representation. The poorer nation or state can continue to rely on its numerical parity or superiority with population even if it suffers deficits in economic activity. If one looks at the least populated state in the United States it is Wyoming with 579,679 persons projected in 2015[13]. The most populated state is California with 38,421,464 persons[14]. If both states are apportioned 2 Senators each regardless of the population, Wyoming has nearly 66x as much proportional representation than California[15]. If one looks at New York, 19,673,174[16] (2015), and Florida, 19,645,772[17] (2015) the leverage is a little more than 34x[18], and the differential in Texas, 26,538,614[19] (2015) at nearly 46x[20]. It is obvious that the residents and citizens of states within the same union are comfortable with different ratios of representation, despite the fact it is not correlated to population, GDP, or taxes remitted back to the federal government.

This presents an opportunity to legitimize GDP based representation by relating the differential in Senatorial representation back to the differential in Gross Domestic Product. Let us examine the GDP of Mexico versus the United States. In 2015, Mexico had a 1.151T[21]

---

[13] "Wyoming, Community Facts", Census.gov, accessed on July 1st, 2017.
https://factfinder.census.gov/faces/nav/jsf/pages/index.xhtml

[14] "California, Community Facts", Census.gov, accessed on July 1st, 2017 at
https://factfinder.census.gov/faces/nav/jsf/pages/index.xhtml

[15] Derivative of California 2015 population estimate / Wyoming 2015 population estimate

[16] "New York, Community Facts", Cenus.gov, accessed on July 1st, 2017.
https://factfinder.census.gov/faces/nav/jsf/pages/index.xhtml

[17] "Florida, Community Facts", Cenus.gov, accessed on July 1st, 2017.
https://factfinder.census.gov/faces/nav/jsf/pages/index.xhtml

[18] Derivative of New York and Florida 2015 population estimates / Wyoming 2015 population estimate (individual)

[19] "Texas, Community Facts", Cenus.gov accessed on July 1st, 2017.
https://factfinder.census.gov/faces/nav/jsf/pages/index.xhtml

[20] Derivative of Texas 2015 population estimates / Wyoming 2015 population estimate

[21] "Mexico GDP", worldbank.org, accessed on July 1st, 2017.

dollar economy compared to the 18.037T dollar GDP of the United States[22]. This is only a ratio of nearly 16x[23]. This representational ratio is nearly one third that of the difference between Senatorial representation between the state of Texas and Wyoming[24]. The representational ratio for Canada with a GDP of 1.553T[25] is nearly 12x[26] which is only a fifth of the nearly 66x ratio between the largest state, California, and the smallest state Wyoming, within the US Senate[27]. The 66x ratio is maintained precisely when a comparison between California's $2,531,304B GDP and Wyoming's $38,357B GDP is made[28].

For better comparisons of representational ratios between Mexico, Canada, and the United States examine the 2015 GDP of California at 2.531T, Texas at 1.592T, New York at 1.447T, and Florida at 0.903T[29]. Mexico has a population of close to 125.9m[30] persons and Canada has 35.84m[31] persons in 2015. In 2015, California had a population of 38.42m[32], Texas has 26.54m[33], Florida has

---

http://data.worldbank.org/indicator/NY.GDP.MKTP.CD?locations=MX

[22] "United States GDP", worldbank.org, accessed on July 1st, 2017.
http://data.worldbank.org/indicator/NY.GDP.MKTP.CD?locations=US&view=chart

[23] Derivative of US 2015 GDP estimates / Mexico 2015 GDP estimate

[24] Representational ratio of Texas/Wyoming and US/Mexico, or 46/16 = 2.875

[25] "California GDP", worldbank.org, accessed on July 1st, 2017.
http://data.worldbank.org/indicator/NY.GDP.MKTP.CD?locations=CA

[26] Derivative of GDP estimate for Canada/ GDP estimate of U.S.

[27] Derivative of California 2015 population estimate / Wyoming 2015 population estimate

[28] "News Releases, Regional GDP by State", bea.gov, accessed on July 1st, 2017.
https://bea.gov/newsreleases/regional/gdp_state/qgsp_ newsrelease.htm

[29] "News Releases, Regional GDP by State", bea.gov, accessed on July 1st, 2017.
https://bea.gov/newsreleases/regional/gdp_state/qgsp_ newsrelease.htm

[30] "Mexico Population Totals", worldbank.org, accessed on July 1st, 2017.
http://data.worldbank.org/indicator/SP.POP.TOTL?locations=MX

[31] "California Population Totals", worldbank.org, accessed on July 1st, 2017.
http://data.worldbank.org/ indicator/SP.POP.TOTL?locations=CA

[32] "California Community Facts", Census.gov, accessed on July 1st, 2017.
https://factfinder.census.gov/faces/nav/jsf/pages/index.xhtml

19.65m[34], and New York has 19.67m[35]. All of the representational ratios fall within reasonable expectation when compared to the U.S. Senate. Canada falls in line with the largest states in the Union presenting no significant deviation in population or GDP. Mexico has a population of nearly 3x that of California[36] and 5x that of Texas[37]. This is high, but Mexico might be split into multiple states to lower the representation ratio. The limited statistical analysis presents a solid argument that GDP is a valid index to base representational coefficients on if one already approves of the differentials in ratios present in Senatorial representation.

Contemporary democracies reliance on senatorial representation opens the rhetorical door for GDP based representation, as it is an arbitrary form of representation not correlated to population on the individual basis but earning an inverse relationship on the aggregate. This is a direct contrast to the positive aspects of representation based on GDP. Gross Domestic Product is a function of the capacity for production in the nation, the availability of natural resources, and the quality of industrial organization. These are critical components in modern society and economy. If legitimate governments are already predicated on the arbitrary representation found in a Senate, then a GDP based system of representation already has enough precedent to make a warrant of legitimacy.

---

[33] "Texas Community Facts", Census.gov, accessed on July 1st 2017.
https://factfinder.census.gov/faces/nav/jsf/pages/index.xhtml
[34] "Florida Community Facts", Census.gov, accessed on July 1st, 2017.
https://factfinder.census.gov/faces/nav/jsf/pages/index.xhtml
[35] "New York Community Facts", Census.gov, accessed on July 1st, 2017.
https://factfinder.census.gov/faces/nav/jsf/pages/index.xhtml
[36] Derivative of Mexico's population of 125.9m / California's population of 38.42m
[37] Derivative of Mexico's population of 125.9m / Texas' population of 26.54m

It is far more effective to develop representational coefficients which moderate the number of representatives in the short term but permit enough flexibility for proportional representation in the long term. Representational coefficients based on Gross Domestic Product generally distribute one vote to each resident satisfying the higher standards of Universal Suffrage. Thus, GDP based representation provides a reform that can negotiate the changing expectations of a population, over periods of instability and tumult. The promise of improved representation will bring parties to the negotiation table and impart patience and discipline in any successful reform movement.

GDP representation must provide opportunities for newly incorporated states to slowly acquire more proportional representation over time, but mature economies must also be able to protect themselves from extreme changes in the electorate during the incorporation process. Mature economies will often have a GDP growth rate large enough to moderate the GDP gains by developing economies even when they have twice the rate of increase. However, the developing nation will be the recipient of federal tax dollars which should hasten the growth rate even more. The distribution of federal tax subsidies along with the institutional power of GDP representation for the more mature economy should bend the developing economy to the institutional standards found in the older more established states.

It is arguable that most interim governments during civil wars or wars for independence should be based on GDP so that they can entice the more capitalized and organized cities into their union prior to or during the conflict. When a democratic union attracts cities, they gain significant GDP for the war effort, they can deny their adversaries tax revenues through tax embargoes, they are a source for new conscripts, they can disrupt supply chains, and cut off trade routes. An interim government may be implicitly temporary but many of the same people pledging support and fealty to the interim government, will be voting on the substance and composition of the permanent government after the war.

When an interim government gives cities and wealthier states more proportional representation during the conflict, it makes it more likely the achieve independence or preserve more of the union after a secession attempt, justifying the outsized influence on the conventions leading up to a more permanent union. In simulations, GDP-based interim governments should routinely outperform demographic-based interim governments when put against adversaries in a dynamic environment where institutional protests like tax riots and debt defaults can change the outcomes in democratic conflicts, and deny authoritarian states tax revenues and supplies, making them far more dangerous to the status quo. Cities are more often more diverse than rural states, making them more important in the conventional process, as it ensures minorities and other vulnerable populations have a voice in establishing a government which would otherwise be dominated by simple majorities by demographic-majorities. Not only are war-time outcomes better, but post-war peace time outcomes should also better satisfy a larger portion of the population in a representative democracy with a diverse electorate.

GDP-based representation aids war efforts by allowing democracies to recruit cities into the union, denying their adversaries the GDP and population bases from the emancipated city. It requires the city to voluntarily ally with the warring democracy but the offer of high-quality voting rights and civil rights with trade incentives should entice a significant portion of the population to join the rebellion. A despotic opponent may have more control over local elections but the invading democracy should have enough expertise in setting up interim governments and supporting resistance movements, that individual cities can be targeted, with coastal cities preferred to interrupt supply chains and trade, or to set up forward operating bases, but anytime a large metropolitan area can be converted into an allied democracy, it will deny the authoritarian or adversarial nation a substantial amount of GDP and conscripts to wage war.

Most contemporary democratization efforts focused on eliminating the federal threat and converting the nation to democracy during occupation, but GDP-based representation allows the democracy to interact with cities more effectively spelling out the terms of unionization more explicitly before any risks are onboarded. Future democratization efforts can focus on emancipated cities, which are the smallest political unit qualifying for sovereignty and inclusion into a republican system of democratic representation. Once a city is incorporated into the democratic union, its citizenry will be more zealous in the fight for freedom or emancipation from the adversarial nation. The benefit to democratic peoples is more limited, considering they already have access to high-quality voting rights, civil rights, and economic opportunities, which is evidenced by the lack of violent conflict between democracies. In more competitive environments, where one democratic nation offers significantly better voting rights and economic benefits, there may some tension between the nations, but the risk from GDP loss after conflict will be priced into the economic benefit of enticing a city or state to change loyalties, eliminating most threats of coercion.

Cities joining a democratic union based on GDP may have lower proportional representation in the GDP chamber after fighting a war for independence, but they will likely be able to have full proportional representation in the demographic chamber. Cities are usually aggregators of GDP, so they capture a disproportionate amount of GDP compared to their state or nation making it much more equitable for them to join the democratic union than if the entire state joined the union. The city captures more proportional representation than if the entire state joined because they would have less implicit control over how they were represented in the union. A city with 50% of the GDP but 20% of the population can lose its political identity to a state with 80% of the population and 50% of the GDP. Most democracies operate through majority rule, allowing the demographic majority to enforce its voting preferences on minorities even when the split is even. A city would recognize this and find emancipation more attractive than remaining complicit in the defense of an authoritarian regime or lower-quality democracy.

With the cities help, the other regions of the nation could be occupied and assimilated, keeping the cultural and economic bonds but not the political bonds. The poorer and more rural regions will still enjoy the democratic union with proportional representation and modest representation in the GDP chamber. It is an equitable relationship for all parties, although cities gain an outsized portion of representation in exchange for their increased utility in war and improved trade with the union. Although democratic unions of using other representational coefficients can assimilate cities and states, GDP-based representation is more effective because the allied cities-states get proportionally more representation in the union while the occupied rural states get proportionally less in one chamber and an equivalent proportion of representation in another.

A major theme of this book is the rural and metropolitan divide. Coastal regions typically have much larger populations than central regions resulting in more economic development. Larger populations tend to be more diverse, better educated, and populations have better economic outcomes. These geo-spatial properties are often far more important than political affiliations. These properties are held constant across different states, nations, and continents. The more densely populated regions on the coasts are the centers of trade allowing them to develop more universities, more industries, and attract a more diverse population. This urban and rural divide permeates most aspects of a nation's culture and political process and is most evident in its fiscal policy. We can look at the United States as an example.

Within the United States, the coastal states pay nearly 57% of the federal taxes and the central and southern states only 43%, for a 14% difference.[38] [39] [40]. Despite the large incongruent contributions to the federal government, the funds are distributed almost equally between two groups of states. In 2015, $1.376T were paid to the coastal states and $1.38T paid to the central and southern states [41]. The two sets of states have an equal

---

[38] "2015 Data Book", IRS.gov, accessed on July 2nd, 2017.
https://www.irs.gov/pub/irs-soi/15databk.pdf
[39] "State Summaries", USAspending.gov, accessed on July 2nd, 2017.
https://www.usaspending.gov/transparency/Pages/StateSummaries.aspx

[41] Derivative of state expenditures from US Census for year 2015 accessed on July 2nd 2017 at https://www.usaspending.gov/transparency/Pages/StateSummaries.aspx

number of residents, with nearly 160 million living on the coasts and 161m living in the central and southern regions. Cost of living is more expensive in the large metropolitan and coastal states, and one would expect their federal subsidies to reflect the increased cost of business in the states[42]. If federal spending was proportional to contributions, those states would receive nearly 1.56T in subsidies while the more rural states would fall to $1.11T in subsides[43].

The coastal states pay 57% of taxes and only receive 50% of subsidies while the central and southern states pay only 43% of taxes and still receive 50% of subsidies[44] [45]. This 14% differential found in both sets equates to a loss of about 2.2% annual GDP economic activity in coastal states and a gain of 2.8% annual GDP in central and southern states[46]. The increased drag on the coastal states has reduced their GDP growth and bolstered GDP growth in the central and southern states. If federal taxes average about 20% of GDP[47], this represents more than $222B[48] GDP difference in economic activity that would be conserved within the

---

[42] Richard Florida "Is life better in Americas red states", Nytimes.com, last modified 01/3/2015. https://www.nytimes.com/2015/01/04/opinion/sunday/is-life-better-in-americas-red-states.html

[43] Multiplied 2015 US Census data on government spending by 57% for blue states and 43% for red states.

[44] "State Summaries", USAspending.gov, accessed on July 7th, 2017. https://www.usaspending.gov/transparency/Pages/StateSummaries.aspx

[45] "2015 Data Book", IRS.gov, accessed on July 2nd, 2017. https://www.irs.gov/pub/irs-soi/15databk.pdf

[46] "News Releases, regional GDP by state", bea.gov, access on July 1st, 2017. https://bea.gov/newsreleases/regional/gdp_state/qgsp_newsrelease.htm

[47] John Gruber, Public finance and public policy (New York, NY: Worth Publishers, 2015), p. 14.

[48] "News Releases, regional GDP by state", bea.gov, access on July 1st, 2017. https://bea.gov/newsreleases/regional/gdp_state/qgsp_newsrelease.htm

coastal states if they received a proportional number of subsidies to taxes paid.

This differential in federal tax contributions and federal tax subsidies has hastened the growth of the central and southern states by a non-trivial amount. According to GDP estimates for 1963 through 1997, the coastal states share of GDP shrank by nearly 0.99% and the central and southern state GDP grew by 0.99%[49]. This produced a total shift in GDP of close to 1.9%[50]. From 1997 to 2015, coastal states shrank nearly 1.15% and the central and southern states grew by 1.15% for a total shift of nearly 2.3%[51]. The rate of GDP growth is accelerating, with the period from 1963-1997 being nearly 3x as long as the period from 1997-2015 despite the gains in GDP being nearly equivalent. The coastal states' share of GDP shrank from nearly 58% to just over 55% and the central and southern states' share grew from 42% to nearly 45%, cutting the difference from nearly 16% to just over 10%.[52] This would translate to significant representational gains for the central and southern states if they were participating in a GDP based political union. Most nations last hundreds of years and in just 52 years, the central and southern states would have gained nearly 6% more proportional representation[53].

This is a selling point for the GDP based political union. Nations can't simply look at their historic GDP

---

49 "News Releases, regional GDP by state", bea.gov, access on July 1st, 2017. https://bea.gov/newsreleases/regional/gdp_state/qgsp_ newsrelease.htm

50 "News Releases, regional GDP by state", bea.gov, access on July 1st, 2017. https://bea.gov/newsreleases/regional/gdp_state/qgsp_ newsrelease.htm

51 "News Releases, regional GDP by state", bea.gov, access on July 1st, 2017. https://bea.gov/newsreleases/regional/gdp_state/qgsp_ newsrelease.htm

52 Derivative of the difference in total proportion of NIAC GDP estimates for 1997-2015 and SIC GDP estimates for 1963-1997, by state party preference.

53 Derivative of the net difference between of NIAC GDP estimates for 1997-2015 and SIC GDP estimates for 1963-1997, by state party preference.

growth independent of the expectation of gaining access to more federal tax subsidy and more favorable trade and investment positions. The union itself should promote faster GDP growth in the less developed parts of the nation, helping accommodate or mitigate the superior representational position of the more developed and wealthier nation. This is the promise; a less developed nation will join a political union with an obviously inferior representational position with the expectation of acquiring perfectly proportional representation when an equivalent per capita GDP is acquired. Political unions and nations are expected to last hundreds of years and small differences in federal tax subsidies should contribute to the evening out of per capita GDP between the states of a single market economy (shared currency and regulatory environment). The expectation of more fluid representation should increase the rate of union formation and improve the democratization movement.

No political union is perfect. Representational deficiencies always exist. The difference in federal tax subsidy for the Northern and West Coast States is likely caused by representational deficiencies found in the Senate. With 56% of the Senate seats from the central and southern states, typically more rural and poorer states, that favor one political party over the other, they have been able to monopolize the appropriations process and diverting huge sums of tax subsidies back to their states[54]. Only 44% of the Senate seats are located within the Coastal states, producing a natural 12% advantage for parties with higher affiliation in the central and southern states[55]. Seats do switch parties but there should be a tendency for one party to win a majority of the elected

---

[54] Derived from state party preferences demonstrated on page 42

[55] Derived from state party preferences demonstrated on page 42

offices in the state, if that state does demonstrate a preference for political affiliation.

Despite the blue states maintaining nearly equal population with the central and southern states[56], they have a 12% deficit in representation. A 12% seat advantage is a serious benefit for one party and an almost insurmountable obstacle for the other. A 12-seat advantage will result in far more Senate majorities for the party with the seat advantage. This is even more true in environments where a filibuster is abused requiring 60 affirmative votes to pass budgetary measures or debt ceilings. Allowing the party to easily obstruct the legislative process in the bicameral legislature. Worse, the political party representing the more rural, poorer, and less educated states can preserve the austerity conditions that produce populist movements, wealth inequality, and political corruption.

The states that prefer austerity measures and weak labor laws will demonstrate a faster GDP growth and can advertise their economic policies as more successful than those that favor higher taxes and higher wages. The politicians will have superficial data that supports their claims that austerity promotes faster GDP growth. However, the data collected from these states is invalid unless it is corrected for the significant amount of economic stimulus provided by the differential in contributions and expenditures. Wealth inequality and austerity produce more poverty, and the worse the poverty in a region, the more federal tax subsidies they receive. This is a counterproductive feedback loop, resulting in more wealth inequality and defunded

---

[56] "2015 Population Tables", Census.gov, accessed on July 3rd, 2017.
https://www.census.gov/data/tables/2016/demo/popest/nation-total.html

governments susceptible to government shutdowns and debt defaults.

GDP based representation can break this feedback loop. The wealthier and better educated states will have more political power and impose their economic policies on the lower GDP states. They can ensure the public has living wages and the government isn't susceptible to debt default threats of government shutdowns. They will support progressive taxes and collective bargaining. The public will make better electoral decisions, once they are elevated above poverty and subsistence living. The improved economic outcomes will provide more support for the political parties advocating for economic reform. A new positive feedback loop towards prosperity and political stability will be formed and the nation can embark on a mission for territorial expansion. The citizens of other nations will seek to adopt the culture and prosperity of the successful democracy and may enter union with it.

Obviously, political unions that incorporate senates will attract different participants than those that support demographic chambers or econometric chambers. New states will consider the representational deficiencies involved with the current political system and seek to exploit them or mitigate them. Nations will make concessions when entering political unions with other nations. This is understandable from the perspective of the more established and developed nation as they benefit from the new labor and consumption markets and should be able to leverage their current representational advantages for the foreseeable future. It is also understandable from the developing nation's perspective, which gains access to larger margins of federal tax subsidy and investment capital. All the nations will benefit from improved security with military benefiting from a larger population base for enlisted, access to the coasts, resources, and better base locations.

Don't forget, econometric representation only offers the promise of improvement. These outcomes may fail to be achieved and all parties bear risk in the unionization process. Wealth inequality is a dominant theme in politics. Even if historic GDP growth rates don't demonstrate a faster rate in the developing states, the fact that growth was distributed evenly among all states is testament to the effectiveness of extra economic stimulation through federal tax subsidies. Economic growth is usually a tautology, wealthier states grow much more wealthy than poorer states. Wealth tends to accumulate unless it is acted directly upon by public policy intended to curb the growing inequality. This is true on the macro-political or state level as much as it is true on the individual or family level. A huge imbalance in federal tax policy might be precisely what enables a poorer state to continue growing at the same rate as the wealthier states. Without the massive imbalance is subsidy, the two political markets would continue to move apart

A nation might agree to unionization expecting a much more rapid growth in GDP but only experiencing static growth compared to the larger market. This is more acceptable if the union includes a Senate that might provide a huge representational advantage to a less populated state. In the United States, the smallest state has nearly 66x as much representation in the institution and the largest state[57]. Under these terms, a less developed nation with a smaller population and lower

---

[57] Comparing California to Wyoming by population constrained by terms of Senate representation.

GDP might still consider unionization with the larger and more developed states. Likewise, a nation with a far larger population but lower GDP will see a benefit in unionization if it gains significant representational advantages in the demographic chamber even if it might not ever acquire a superior position in the econometric chamber. These are tradeoffs in the political markets politicians will weigh during unionization negotiations (post conflict or peaceful).

This difference in situational preference creates a more competitive market for unionization. If two nations are aggressively pursuing peaceful expansion and one offers an econometric chamber paired with a demographic chamber and the other offers an economic chamber paired with a Senate, each nation will attract different consumers. When two competing nations offer the same client different options, that client can examine growth rates in population and GDP and determine which is a more equitable relationship for them to pursue. They won't compete over the same cliental because the cliental will have their own agenda and seek to maximize their own political power within the union.

These calculations shouldn't be underweighted in terms of likelihood of occurring, when one examines the relatively short period during which both the U.S. and E.U. were formed and those conditions that enabled the two unions to thrive. Environmental and economic conditions in the near future might promote more expansion in democratic nations. These are optimal outcomes. More mixed outcomes should be expected. The history of the world includes periods of colonialism and imperialism where democratic nations have participated. It is a reasonable expectation that the world enters another period of aggressive expansion and integration but where innovations in political representation ensure that democratic culture and rights are protected against more authoritarian regimes.

There is an implicit degree of trust when forming imperial democracies. The newly incorporated states must believe the intent of the host states to achieve equilibrium in per capita GDP and distribute representation more uniformly in the union. If the States with the higher GDP abuse their institutional power by withholding federal tax subsidies while exporting austerity measures, regressive tax policies, and deregulate labor conditions they can preserve the low representational conditions for new states. This breaks the covenant, resulting in economic instability and political instability, and it could destroy the Union. The new state will rely on support from opposition parties within the more nature economies and relentlessly protest the conditions. If peacefulresistance fails, the developing state could shrug off the imperial ties, like so many other states have in the past by taking up arms against their oppressors. The promise of proportional representation must be honored, or ruin will follow negligent leadership.

To acquire a more representative government, member states will pursue economic reforms that distribute incomes more evenly, federalist subsidies more equally, and obligations more equitably. This tendency will promote a movement towards higher legislative production rates and higher quality laws. When economic conditions are corrected, the improved conditions will make future reforms more likely. Success breeds more success. When reforms are denied, it immediately elicits calls of corruption, oppression, and exploitation directly related to under representation. This can result in cultures that support rebellion or secession, undermining the productivity of the union. These conditions may make economic reform less likely as the electorate splits into partisan divides and can't reach compromises as easily.

Democratic governments need to be validated by popular support otherwise the public can start to distrust it and resist its taxes and laws. This is a dangerous situation, especially during demographic shifts and periods of wealth inequality. Economic data must be reported accurately. Reporting integrity must be ensured with an agency auditing tax data, firm accounting, and state level aggregation to ensure that all GDP figures are accurate. Newly incorporated states must have complete faith in the reporting of financial data before they agree to the political union. Firms and corporations must report their accounting data promptly and accurately. Strong institutions are a necessary component of democracy. This includes reporting laws with universal application, integrity in form, and fully enforced. The accuracy of the audits will be a strong inducement for unionization.

If the reporting isn't standardized, states will not trust each other and disrupt the economy and due process. The suspicion will invite fear and anger into the union. This isn't easily cured. In the worst-case scenarios, the states fearing exploitation will organize with other states and there will be secession or war. In the best-worst case scenario, the imperial democracy is viewed as corrupt. It won't be able to advertise its culture or political process as a benefit. It won't be able to effectively incorporate new states into the union and in more competitive environments, it will be eclipsed by larger states with larger economies. Trust is the most important component of a relationship between new states and older states. It is the cornerstone of GDP based representation.

3 GDP ELECTORATES

Wars are inevitable. It would be a productive innovation to develop a system for the integration of electorates rather than simply the occupation of other nations. The inhibitions on rapidity expanding an electorate that includes different ethnicities, religions, and cultures will still be in place. If put to a popular vote, many of the citizens might reject the incorporation of a state into the union. This doesn't mean the country won't defend itself with war, but it will moderate the number of conflicts by reducing the likelihood of coercion into a union. Wars are usually counter-productive and wasteful. The misery that accompanies them is unrivaled and rarely justified. However, war is a common response to adverse conditions and no matter how terrible the consequences, it will be rationalized as an acceptable strategy.

The destructive consequences of war should be severe enough to discourage most aggressive imperial tendencies. It is doubtful nations will embark on risk expansionist policies, if it destroys the economy of the regions and destabilizes all the participants. Populations usually resist long wars with high casualties and forced conscription. This is dangerous for any democracy. Government may acquire substantial debts related to the war expenditures, making them susceptible to debt defaults or government shutdowns. They could see their labor forces decimated, and their natural resources spoiled. Democratic expansion may not justify these risks. There are financial and political incentives to unionization, even after occupation and conflict, but the equation isn't balanced. Used defensively, democratic imperialism is productive, but nations will have to account for the full range of possibilities and consequences of conflict prior to the adventure.

Democratic imperialism is much more likely to occur within a region with a similar culture and equivalent economic development. Not only do they have more religious sympathies but inclusion within a political system with GDP based representation will implicitly be more equitable. It's far less likely that a mature economy in Europe incorporates a state in Africa than it is for a democratic state in Africa to consider expanding their electorate through incorporating neighbors. The same is true in Asia and South America. The net consequences of this tendency could be an acceleration of the democratization process with a scaling of nations into larger free trade zones more able to defend themselves against authoritarian threats.

This doesn't constrain a democratic empire to its own region or continent. Modern transport and communication make it possible for a nation to incorporate a state that is not contiguous or on another continent. Democratic imperialism is still dependent on voluntary participation. No people or state can be easily coerced into union even during an occupation. The newly incorporated state must see equity and value in the statehood. This is far more likely within regions that share religion and culture, but proximity is not always necessary. Don't forget that the primary driver of expansion will be voluntary and peaceful negotiations between neighbors for free trade zones and political unions. The number of opportunities is unbound compared to those of war. War is a far less effective means to expand an electorate. The populations will be less willing, and the economy will require far more rehabilitation after the conflict. Most of the benefits from imperial expansion are gained through peaceful integration. Neighboring states have many more opportunities to form productive relationships with a strong tendency towards cooperation and voluntary union.

Conservative populations will be more susceptible to the rhetoric of econometric representation based on GDP. Culturally, Conservatives tend to trust free market ideologies and institutions found in the private sector. They will offer less resistance to the premise of econometric representation. They are often business owners or professionals who are fluent in economic concepts like Gross Domestic Product, Free Trade, and Market Economy. This familiarity is an incentive. It also helps that the representation is variable and where expertise and patience can increase their political power outside of any immigration or demographic movements. This coincides with many beliefs in fierce individuality and the idea that effort can overcome any obstacle or deficiency.

Conservatives will be more comfortable with both sides of the representational equation. They will accept less representation up front for the promise of proportional representation later. Business owners have a different perspective than employees or other professionals. They stand to gain more from uninhibited trade and have more material wealth making them less susceptible to economic disruptions. Business owners have more innate political power by virtue of their extra capitalization. All governments seem to recognize firms more readily than individuals. Wealthier firms have significant institutional advantages over poorer firms or individuals. The political caste sees an advantage to cultivate relationships with industrials and wealthy people. This all contributes to surplus political power and an incentive for business owners to accept the unequal conditions of GDP based representation.

This is especially true when the business owners are in developing economies that will benefit from a political union with a more mature economy. The developing economy will receive far more in federal subsidies than it contributes to in taxes, and it will be business owners who primarily benefit. The business owners will be the vendors earning such contracts for services provided to the new government. Higher paid employees contribute to more consumption for businesses. The lower labor costs could improve exports to a more mature economy. Business owners will have the most incentive to support a political union with more mature economies. This could be motivation for regime change in authoritarian nations and could accelerate the conversion rate of despotic or communist countries.

GDP based representation offers conservatives the opportunity to support a representation that closely identifies with their culture of business acumen while not trespassing on any long-standing thresholds for accurate and honest representation. GDP based representation comports to the contemporary standards in democracy for universal suffrage. Econometric representation has more appeal when it delivers high quality democratic entitlements that don't deviate from this ideal.

Conservatives can finally declare support for a high-quality system of political representation based on Economy.

Recruiting conservatives into a democratization movement focused on wealth-based representation will benefit the entire community by inviting a highly motivated and energetic population into the cause for universal suffrage and high-quality democratic entitlements. This will implicitly reduce the support received by non-democratic governments. Despots and tyrants are dependent on loyalist populations and wealth-based systems of representation might interrupt this relationship. Econometric representation is in a language that business leaders understand and if confidence in the establishment can be shaken or diverted, it could cause larger populations to defect towards democratization.

GDP based representation may be critical for nation building in less developed nations. The owners class and investors class are typically involved in the more successful revolutions or regime changes. They will be attracted to the theory and the rhetoric used. The more developed regions may acquire more political power, resulting in more predictable and stable outcomes. There is an implicit legitimacy in GDP when economic activity is weakly correlated to education and population density. These characteristics often make for more sustainable and durable democracies. They also enjoy more capital support for the new government. The regions with the highest GDP will provide more proportional tax revenues. They will have more labor to draw on for public works and enlistment in the armed forces. GDP based representation confers several advantages to the fledgling democracy that may improve its chances for survival.

Even small improvements in support result in significant improvements in the odds for regime change when the affected populations are in the millions and billions. It is the law of large numbers. If a regime oppresses or upsets just a small number of its citizenry with abuses in civil liberties or due process, a segment of the disaffected public will quickly radicalize organize to protect the civil liberties like free press or the right to peacefully organize. As the number of abuses grows, so will the support for the democratization movement, representing a larger number of activists and more financial support. More importantly, it constricts the current regimes access to labor and capital. There are two sides to the single frame, one results in a gain for activists and rebels, and the other a loss of support for the loyalist, with the improvement in the odds of success squared.

Choices are always made from available options, not the ideal. The decision is evaluated through a comparison to the ideal, but that ideal is rarely satisfied during a crisis. A people may accept lower quality democratic entitlements with the expectation of acquiring a more ideal state at a future point. This was true in the early democracies which often resembled aristocracy with restricted electorates. Most improvements are earned by incremental reforms through the political process. The property that makes incremental reform most likely, is universal suffrage and a diverse electorate. With honest and accurate representation, a people will slowly acclimate to the diversity in economic outcomes, religion, and ethnicity found in most nations. Debate and peaceful protest will frame the civil rights and economic issues while the democratic process produces an opportunity to pass laws protecting their interests. GDP representation provides the basis for incremental reform.

It is an immediate concession in quality of representation with the expectation of future entitlement.

Demographic representation provides an ideal form of government in most circumstances. It has the full authority and legitimacy of majority control. Proportional distribution allocates votes on an individual basis through universal suffrage, overcoming natural boundaries like region and statehood. It is easily understood and counted. It is also predictable. It is implicit that the candidates with the most supporters win most of the elections. It is imperative that the most popular policies are debated in the legislature, evaluated by the bureaucracy, and studied in academia. However, there are always those minority groups and classes that will strive to check the unbridled populism of a majority. Politicians fear populism and populism can be checked by introducing a legislative chamber decoupled from demographic representation.

This demand has historically been satisfied by the senates, but the GDP chamber is more adept in this role. GDP is only weakly correlated to population (within states in a single market economy) but it still carries the potential for proportional representation when per capita GDP is equally distributed across all states. GDP can be both separate from popular representation and equivalent. This introduces a controlled measure of inefficiency into a durable political process. It actively checks populism by empowering the states with the most GDP (wealth) and therefore the least susceptibility to the animal spirits. Legislative chambers based on GDP are a more effective complement to demographic chambers than Senates. GDP imparts more value than an arbitrary assignment of representation like that found in the senate.

GDP based representation is more dynamic than senatorial representation. When GDP is positively correlated to population through more equal per capita GDP, it provides the more educated and more expert population with more proportional representation in both the demographic chamber and the GDP based chamber. However, this relationship is inverted when it comes to political unions with less developed countries. Less developed nations will have few lower per capita GDP and representation will be less correlated to population. This is an important concept when striking the agreement for an economic zone or Union. The GDP chamber acts as a foil to the demographic chamber without completely negating the benefit of proportional representation.

GDP based representation offers better outcomes than senates for most political unions. In larger nations, senates often create the conditions for populism. It will be the more numerous and smaller states that acquire a disproportionate amount of political power in the chamber. Smaller states are generally poorer (with lower per capita GDP) and less educated, making them more resistant to change and reform. Once the economic conditions deteriorate, the shorter term of a demographic chamber will make it more susceptible to the populist spirits. A senate's use of a filibuster can then preserves the poor economic conditions that moved the public to the violent throws of populism and nativism.

The senate's inverse relationship to population is counterproductive. It is often unnecessary that a bicameral legislature is the best bulwark against populism. Setting two institutions on opposed election schedules is the most effective means to temper popular sentiment in the moment. Increasing the terms of the candidates will insulate them from populism, while an increased number of elections will improve the institutions responsiveness to contemporary conditions. It is counter-productive to diminish the legitimacy of majority rule by inserting a Senate. A bicameral process can be easily obstructed, especially when senates so often benefit the poorer states who invariably support populist candidates The GDP chamber accomplishes the same anti-populist goal while providing a pathway to proportional representation after per capita GDP equilibrates throughout the union. In both respects, the GDP based system of representation is a higher order form of organization in nations and for states.

In an environment of political instability resulting from climate change and wealth inequality, democracies can protect themselves from more frequent conflicts and conquests by democratic imperialism. There will be resources shortages, economic disasters, immigration and demographic shifts all contributing to poverty, strife, and war. Democracies can put themselves in a position to better defend themselves by incorporating other states and nations into the political union. They can transmit the successes of democracy through their constitutions, their institutions, and their culture to protect those new entitlements for the fledgling states.

Wealth based representation provides an exceptional opportunity for a resurgence in the democratization movement when conservative with populations around the world can identify with a political process that more accurately reflects their preferences and ambitions while satisfying their requirements for universal suffrage and high-quality Democratic standards. Wealth based representation will attract more support from business owners and conservatives who might otherwise support the current non-democratic establishment as loyalists. This will result in more frequent regime change, and a gradient towards democracy. Not all movements will be successful, but even failed efforts will impart a culture and preference for democracy in the despotic state.

Any innovation in political rhetoric or process that increases the odds of successfully converting a non-democratic nation into a Democratic nation is a permanent and significant improvement in the democratization movement. This is how we establish civil society and build a durable and equitable civilization. It is homesteading. It is establishing that outpost in the wilderness. GDP based representation is one of these innovations. Economy and finance are our immediate environments. They are an all-powerful force in our lives whether a culture or individual is compliant, or whether they rally against the general inequities and the waste created. The economy is unavoidable. GDP based representation harnesses the raw power of economy for the body politic. It makes the nation more efficient in terms of representing its own people, and it makes the state more compatible with other states. It is a variable form of representation that accommodates multiple outcomes over many periods.

GDP based representation is an implicit improvement in political science due to its ability to adjust to changing circumstances. This isn't true of senatorial representation. The senate is fixed. Its representational coefficients can change over time with population shifts coercing an inverse movement in leverage but otherwise the number of representatives is fixed and unmoving. This looks prolapsed compared to the use of GDP as a representational coefficient. GDP will generally scale up with population, but it will also increase when more appropriate economic policies are passed. This promises smaller and less developed nations of a more equitable future with GDP based representation. With hard work, patience, and expertise, a state can slowly and incrementally increase its representation of the union. This is for the benefit of the union too. If the state has more successful economic policies, it should have more representation with the opportunity to export them.

Majority rule is still the ideal. It doesn't have to mean a perfectly representational government that has a 100% legislative production rate. Too much efficiency can be counterproductive. A party could pass laws that advantage them during elections permitting them to easily preserve their majority political power. This wouldn't result in honest and accurate political representation. This is the primary drive for introducing a bicameral process. Nations may also impose conditions like a Presidential Veto or a filibuster. However, the framers must make it possible for a people to regulate themselves and govern themselves. If a political process is obstructed too easily it will result in oppression, exploitation, and political instability.

The raw probability (potential) of passing laws in a bicameral legislature is 50% with all things being equal (*perfectly competitive and binary electoral process*). Using the United States as a model, the probability falls to just 25% after a Presidential Veto is applied. However, the probability of passing laws drops to less than 9.5% in environments where the filibuster is abused and a 60-seat margin in the Senate is necessary[58]. These periods can

---

[58] Divided by number of times 60 seat margin in Senate overcome since 1933, where the House and President were all of the same party. "Visual Guide: The Balance of Power Between Congress and the President" Accessed on 7.8.2017. http://wiredpen.com/resources/political-commentary-and-analysis/a-visual-guide-balance-of-power-congress-presidency/

last 40 years of more[59] resulting in increased wealth inequality and stagnant wages[60] [61].

Rarely can a bill pass without the implicit consent of the opposition party. The public almost invariably overestimates the effectiveness of the opposition party because it is so easy to obstruct government and prevent laws from passing. This looks like effectiveness. It looks like expertise, and it attracts those that are susceptible to power and abuse. It also makes the party lobbying for economic reform or political reform a lot less effective. It makes them look weaker and uncoordinated. These are illusions; ninety percent of the force behind the outcome is purely mechanical work from an inefficient and unrepresentative government.

This is extremely dangerous. The political system passes significant laws so infrequently that it is prone to corrections and catastrophe. The crisis then presents an opportunity for cults of personality to form around parties used to bullying or abusing the underrepresented populations like minorities, women, children, and laborers. This tendency was documented in the Stanford Prison Experiment and applies to macro politics as well. The culture is already present. The policies are already widely accepted, and as economic conditions get worse the rhetoric becomes more strained. It is in the vacuum of

---

[59] Tom Donnely and Jeffry Rosen, "Political polarization killed the filibuster", Theatlantic.com. Last modified 4/8/2018.
https://www.theatlantic.com/politics/archive/ 2017/04/ political-polarization-killed-the-filibuster/522360/

[60] Angela Monaghan, "Wealth inequality top 01 worth as much as bottom 90", Theguardian.com, last modified 11/13/2014.https://www.theguardian.com /business/2014/nov/13/us-wealth-inequality-top-01-worth-as-much-as-the-bottom-90

[61] Lawrence Mishel, Elise Gould, and Jose Bivens, "Wage stagnation in nine charts", www.edpi.org, last modified 1/6/2015.http://www.epi.org/publication/charting-wage-stagnation/

remedy through the political process that nightmares are born.

The Europeans nations avoided this fate because of the Parliamentary process. Their executive is appointed by the majority party in their representative legislature, with an almost 50% chance of having alignment in the senate (*in a perfectly competitive and binary electoral system*). This permits a coalition to identify issues and immediately address them with public policy. This doesn't mean the European states are invulnerable to wealth inequality and electoral deficiencies like Gerrymandering and private campaign finance, but it does make it far less likely to aggravate. They are more likely to use public policy to address critical issues than force.

Their second-generation democracies only reduce the risk of compromise. It doesn't complete exclude the risk of crisis. Over the centuries, they have developed long histories of abuse and demographic violence[62]. Their proximity and population density make conflicts more likely, and probably more violent. Prior to 1945, Europe had many of the bloodiest wars[63] . Since 1945, most of the genocides and conflicts were outside of Europe[64]. The greater number of European countries certainly increases the chance of an outbreak, but the more representative government and more efficient government provides as much an inoculation as possible.

---

[62] "European Wars and Battles", Thoughtco.com, accessed on 7/10/2017. https://www.thoughtco.com/european-wars-and-battles-4133312

[63] Jennifer Rosenberg, "The Major wars and conflicts of the 20th century", Thoughtco.com, last modified on 8/13/2018. https://www.thoughtco.com/major-wars-and-conflicts-20th-century-1779967

[64] "Genocides, Politicides, and Other Mass Murder since 1945", Genocidewatch.net, accessed on 7/12/2017. http://genocidewatch.net/genocide-2/genocide-and-politicide/

Low legislative production rates aren't the only threat. Climate change has already occurred. With it will come political instability from rapid environmental changes. Populations will be on the move, and this will disrupt the economy and alter electorates. Automation and the computer era may produce more unemployment and more disparate wealth accumulation[65] These are the conditions where discontent breeds conflict and violence[66]. It is where the spores of dangerous rhetoric spread. The poor economic outcomes and worse political outcomes will make reform necessary but less likely as populations lose confidence in due process. Their judgment will be compromised making them more susceptible to worse decisions.

A people could retreat into empires based on value voting and the ancient instinct to rely on an aristocracy. It may not be just a few years of bad outcomes that can be corrected with term limits and off cycle elections. This could be 400 years or more of decline and instability while humans acclimate to the new conditions. No doubt, there should be a flight to more representative and efficient government, but people generally don't think well during prolonged crises. Instead, they succumb to the same fear and loathing of generations before them and organize into authoritarian systems that promise security and stability but only produce misery.

Nations with higher quality democratic entitlements will be able to protect themselves better.

---

[65] Aaron Frank, "Could automation lead to chronic unemployment? Andrew Mcafee sounds the alarm", forbes.com, last modified 7/19/2012 https://www.forbes.com/sites/singularity/2012/07/19/could-automation-lead-to-chronic-unemployment-andrew-mcafee-sounds-the-alarm/#60603fda1a31

[66] "The economics of violence", economist.com, last modified 4/14/2011 http://www.economist.com/node/18558041

Democratic governance makes a people less likely to conquer other nations for sport, power, prestige, or treasures. This should decrease the frequency and intensity of conflicts just as European conflicts have decreased since 1945[67]. However, when attacked they could defend themselves from invaders and despoilers, and possibly expand their electorate to include the conquered peoples. There is safety in larger numbers. Imperial democracies should have higher GDP and larger populations to marshal during periods of war. There is also safety in representative government. The allure of democratic votes could effectively coerce enemy combatants to surrender more easily. It could improve the conditions for people living under hostile and non-democratic regimes. It certainly provides more stability after a conflict with the hostile population now successfully placated.

---

[67] Jennifer Rosenberg, "The Major wars and conflicts of the 20th century", Thoughtco.com, last modified on 8/13/2018. https://www.thoughtco.com/major-wars-and-conflicts-20th-century-1779967

4 GDP SIMULATIONS

There is some evidence that imposing independence and democracy on a formerly despotic nation does not work with a high enough success rate to justify the process. It could be argued that nation building would be far more effective if formerly despotic nations were incorporated within larger democracy rather than be made independent. These nations could slowly adopt the culture of democracy while still under the stewardship of the conquering nation. It is a better guarantee of due process and strong civil liberties. It is also an incentive for democracies to aggressively pursue nation building in regions or areas where democracy is still under-represented.

If a democratic nation can export its culture and its political process it makes its environment far less dangerous. It is a form of homesteading. Neighbors will be more trustworthy and less hostile. The democratic process makes conflict less likely, but when it is inevitable, they can convert the offender to democracy. This promotes a geometric growth in positive outcomes. As the imperial democracy expands, it will discourage possible invaders, and make wars of conquest less likely. The more it defends itself, the less likely future conflict occurs. This creates a strong tendency towards peace and prosperity. Imperial democracy makes it more likely the culture and expertise involved in the democratic process survives the dangerous and inhospitable conditions created by climate change and wealth inequality.

The democratization movement would be accelerated and improved if mature democracies started incorporating electorates from formerly despotic or communist nations. Democracies tend to be more peaceful and more stable. Despotic nations tend to suffer from internal instability and engage in warlike behavior more often. This will establish a trend in the democratization movement towards expanding the size of democracies, thus the proportion of populations protected by them in the world. Democracies rarely go to war with other democracies but when they do, they can be guaranteed to preserve their democratic entitlements with an emphasis on universal suffrage.

Democratization through expanding electorates, may be sounder than installing democracies in individual states that have not developed the institutions or culture to support them. Democracy isn't always secure or stable, and younger less experienced states are at greater risk of failing. The efforts of the United States in Iraq and Afghanistan are in question. Both states have suffered insults to their system, including civil wars, secessions, and abject corruption. It could be argued that if they were incorporated into a larger, more secure and stable democracy, the fledgling nations would thrive instead of floundering.

The population data and economic data on Iraq and Afghanistan can be used to peer into what the result of this processes will look like. It is understandable that most people will initially object to this exercise based on ethical concerns, but the notion of growth is critical when comparing different representational coefficients.

Iraq and Afghanistan were simply the last two examples of large-scale war efforts made by the United States. It should also be understood that societies change over time, economies change over time, and environments change over time. It is expected that smaller populations incorporated into larger more moderate positions have then tendency to moderate over time. The future is unknown, and this represents an opportunity for both nations involved in the conflict.

In the 1980's Iraq had a population of 13 million[68] and a GDP of 53.4[69] billion. By 2015 Iraq had a population of 36[70] million and a GDP of 168[71] billion. This represents nearly a 276% increase in population and a 314% increase in GDP. These figures can be used to estimate the total change in representation if it were included in a political union with the United States after the last war.

The other conflict involved Afghanistan. In the 1980's Afghanistan had 13 million citizens [72] and 3.6 billion dollars in GDP[73]. By 2015 Afghanistan had 32 million citizens[74] and 19.19 billion dollars in GDP[75]. This

---

[68] "Iraq GDP", Worldbank.org, accessed on July 14, 2017.
http://data.worldbank.org/indicator/NY.GDP. MKTP.CD?locations=IQ
[69] "Iraq Population", Worldbank.org, accessed on July 14, 2017.
http://data.worldbank.org/indicator/ SP.POP.TOTL ?locations=IQ
[70] "Iraq Population", Worldbank.org, accessed on July 14, 2017.
http://data.worldbank.org/indicator/ SP.POP.TOTL ?locations=IQ
[71] "Iraq GDP", Worldbank.org, accessed on July 14, 2017.
http://data.worldbank.org/indicator/NY.GDP. MKTP.CD?locations=IQ
[72] "Afghanistan Population", Worldbank.org, accessed on July 14, 2017.
http://data.worldbank.org/indicator/ SP.POP.TOTL?locations=AF
[73] "Afghanistan GDP", Worldbank.org, accessed on July 14, 2017.
http://data.worldbank.org/indicator/NY. GDP.MKTP.CD?locations=AF
[74] "Afghanistan Population", Worldbank.org, accessed on July 14, 2017.
http://data.worldbank.org/indicator/ SP.POP.TOTL?locations=AF
[75] "Afghanistan GDP", Worldbank.org, accessed on July 14, 2017.
http://data.worldbank.org/indicator/NY. GDP.MKTP.CD?locations=AF

represents a 246% growth in population and a 533% growth in GDP. These figures appear as though they would have significantly more growth and would jeopardize the political power of the United States if they were included with in the electorate, but this simply isn't true.

The United States had a population of 227.25 million citizens[76] in the 1980's and a GDP of $2863B[77]. By 2015 the population had grown to 321.4 million persons with a 141% increase in total citizenship[78]. By 2015 the United States GDP had grown to $17.947T with a 626% increase in value[79].

Although, the United States had slower population growth than both Iraq and Afghanistan, it had a much faster economic expansion. This would help preserve the majority political power of the United States. One must consider the fact that both Iraq and Afghanistan had disproportionately smaller economies than the United States. The ratio of representation would be nearly 53:1 in favor of the United States over Iraq in the 1980's and then grow to nearly 107:1 in 2015. The ratio is even larger for Afghanistan with the ratio being 795:1 in 1980 and 935:1 in 2015.

These outweigh even the largest representational deficiencies in the United States Senate when comparing the states of Vermont or Wyoming to Texas or California. Iraq and Afghanistan would be protected under a

---

[76] "United States Population", Worldbank.org, accessed on July 14, 2017. http://data.worldbank.org/indicator/ SP.POP.TOTL?locations=US

[77] "United States GDP", Worldbank.org, accessed on July 14, 2017. http://data.worldbank.org/indicator/NY. GDP.MKTP.CD?locations=US

[78] "United States Population", Worldbank.org, accessed on July 14, 2017. http://data.worldbank.org/indicator/ SP.POP.TOTL?locations=US

[79] "United States GDP", Worldbank.org, accessed on July 14, 2017. http://data.worldbank.org/indicator/NY. GDP.MKTP.CD?locations=US

"Method of Equal Proportion" leveraging their minimal economic output to one seat in a chamber of just a few hundred legislators[80].   In this respect, they would be elevated to the same standing as Vermont or Wyoming are in the House of Representatives within the United States. Each of these states receive just one representative due to their lack of residents. They receive nearly 0.25% of total representation which should nearly equivalent to the same 0.25% of total representation Iraq or Afghanistan would receive in a GDP based system, if based on a 435-seat chamber[81] [82]

The total proportion of demographic representation for Afghanistan, Iraq, and the United States can be extrapolated from the available figures. Referencing the World Bank 2015 figures, Afghanistan would command only 8.2% of the popular vote, Iraq would gain only 9.2%, and the US would maintain the majority with nearly 83% of the popular vote[83]. Even, when taken together, the two Middle Eastern states will represent only 17% of the total demographic representation in the nation[84]. The United States could effectively protect its majority position for decades and generations to come.

The total proportion of econometric representation for Afghanistan, Iraq and the United States can be projected from current figures. Afghanistan has

---

[80] "Population apportionment", Census.gov, accessed on July 14, 2017.
https://www.census.gov/population/apportionment/about /computing.html

[81] "The house explained", house.gov, accessed on July 14, 2017.
https://www.house.gov/the-house-explained

[82] Derivative of the demographic data on U.S., Afghanistan, and Iraq from
http://data.worldbank.org/

[83] Derivative of the demographic data on U.S., Afghanistan, and Iraq from
http://data.worldbank.org/

[84] Derivative of the demographic data on U.S., Afghanistan, and Iraq from
http://data.worldbank.org/

only 0.01% of total economic output while Iraq had 0.09% of GDP[85]. The United States would almost completely monopolize the political power of the econometric chamber despite losing 17% of representation in the demographic chamber[86].

Iraq had a 4% net gain in demographic representation compared to a net loss of 0.9% in GDP based representation[87]. Afghanistan had a 3% gain in demographic representation and a 0.01% loss in GDP based representation[88]. The United States had a loss of 7% in demographic representation and a gain of 0.09% in GDP based representation[89]. These are stable trajectories for representation within a political union. The fears one population might have from losing sovereignty to another population aren't founded when constrained to a 35-year period. The ratios of total representational proportions also look promising for the new and improved Union.

After 70 years of current demographic representational trends, the United States would only lose another 14% of total proportional representation, leaving it 69% of overall demographic representation[90]. Any fears of loss of majority political power are unfounded, especially when offset by a dominant position in the econometric chamber with no trends suggesting long

---

[85] Derivative of the GDP data on U.S., Afghanistan, and Iraq from
http://data.worldbank.org/

[86] Derivative of the GDP data on U.S., Afghanistan, and Iraq from
http://data.worldbank.org/

[87] Comparison of demographic data and GDP data for U.S., Afghanistan, and Iraq
from http://data.worldbank.org/

[88] Comparison of demographic data and GDP data for U.S., Afghanistan, and Iraq
from http://data.worldbank.org/

[89] Comparison of demographic data and GDP data for U.S., Afghanistan, and Iraq
from http://data.worldbank.org/

[90] Comparison of demographic data and GDP data for U.S., Afghanistan, and Iraq
from http://data.worldbank.org/

term changes in proportion. In 70 years, civil society and equitable economy could reform the more evangelical or extremist components of the new electorate. The democratic institutions of media and freedoms of speech and organization would allow the newly incorporated electorate to develop a culture of integration within the new political union.

The simulations found in this section are based on histories that don't include the extra stimulus provided by federal subsidies. It is expected that many of the states involved have smaller populations and developing economies and would benefit from a surplus of federal investment. This could alter the expected growth in representation within the econometric chamber. More federal subsidies will hasten the speed of economic development with the expectation of more equitable distribution of representation in the GDP chamber. The federal tax subsidy will allow the occupying nation to financially engineer the newly incorporated state, remaking it in the image of itself. The business networks, improved employment and profitability, and improved civil liberties will help inculcate the new culture into the culture of the larger electorate.

Make no mistake. Seeking to expand the electorate by war is a worse strategy than peaceful negotiation and economic integration. Not only is it more likely to be exposed to poorer partners if war is used for expansion, but using violence on persons with similar policy preferences, ethnicities, and religions will only sharpen those sectarian divides that do persist. Trade should be the basis of most political integration. Regulatory systems can be integrated through treaties. Economic unions can become free travel zones and currency zones. International law enforcement agencies can overcome the conventional boundaries of borders. There are few differences outside of regulation, law enforcement, free movement of labor and commerce, and unified currency. It is only a matter of regressing political markets and making elections compatible.

The choice for imposing a demographic form of representation in Iraq was a poor one. For decades, a minority of Sunni had preserved authoritarian control over the Shia majority population. To make matters worse, a highly independent Kurd minority was also present. The United States had decided to impose a Parliamentarian government with demographic representational coefficients. The United States thought it was organizing Iraq for optimal success, but it did not recognize the long history of sectarian tensions. The result was a civil war followed by sectarian violence[91]. This was not the fault of government architects. Parliamentarian governments were far more efficient than Presidential governments (with vetoes and filibusters) and their decision was constrained by the options available to them.

There are better options. Nations with extreme sectarian tensions or predictable demographic shifts may be served better by non-demographic systems of representation. GDP based representation satisfies this condition. It decouples political power from population, minimizing the aggregate political power awarded to populations with numerical superiority. Demographic majorities still have tremendous political power in GDP based representational systems, but non-majority demographic groups have more minority political power.

---

[91] Zana Khasraw, "Who is responsible for Iraq's sectarian violence", last modified June 7, 2013. https://www.opendemocracy.net/zana-khasraw-gul/who-is-responsible-for-iraq%e2%80%99s-sectarian-violence

Demographic representation also permits class-based representation by splitting nations in "haves" and "have nots".

Class based representation may be superior to demographic representation in that the sectarian interest groups are all dissected along above GDP and below GDP lines. Regardless of ethnicity or religion, the nation will be split into Urban populations and Rural populations. This should diffuse some of the anger, angst, or mistrust that divides the sectarian groups. Class division based on incomes and tax liabilities will be successful if they can be adequately justified by the elite and academic interest groups designing the political system. The occupying power should be fluent in the representational technologies to enhance the nation building phase of the war. Econometric representation will contribute to far better outcomes for fledgling democracies than those that have been achieved with demographic representation.

By far the best option is to integrate the nation into an established democracy that is stable and sound enough in economy to sustain the fledgling democracy. The sectarian interest groups will be absorbed into the larger and more diverse nation. However, if that nation also supports a class-based system of representation it will provide a much more secure environment for the incorporated state. The sectarian aspects of the society will be divided along class-based line and then integrated into a larger community with similar divisions. Economy is all important. It encompasses most aspects of life and the sectarian properties of regional affiliation, ethnicity, and religion will be secondary to class based decisions.

Often sectarian tensions contribute to economic disparities and wealth inequality. Class based representation will improve the likelihood of addressing these core problems without invoking tribalism. The economic reforms should cut across multiple demographic groups making it more likely to pass a median partition. Otherwise, the majority demographic groups will vote along tribal or sectarian lines and contribute to austerity measures and exploitative labor policies. If the nation can address these inequities, it is far more likely to succeed as a democracy. If the high unemployment and wage inequality is persistent, minority demographic groups may take adversarial positions and be more susceptible to secessionist or rebellious rhetoric. Class based representation improved the odds of success regardless of whether the nation is incorporated into another electorate, or it is a standalone.

It is obvious that demographic representation has some major vulnerabilities that can be exploited by sectarian interest groups. However, they are still highly effective when stable and most of the optimal outcomes from the democratization movement included demographic based systems. Demographic systems of representation impart a high-quality voter entitlement with universal suffrage and aspects of majority rule. However, occupied nations should be able to choose from a number of options and those options should include econometric representation and class-based representation. Let the nation choose for itself the dominant virtues and characteristics of their democratic form of government. It is a form of empowerment for the fledgling democracy. It results in their identity and is a major determinant of culture. Often, it's not a binary choice between either demographic or econometric systems of representation. Compromise can be made with bicameral legislatures or more complex systems. They can have both.

Class based representation has one profound advantage over demographic representation. Demographic tensions are typically resolved with restricted entitlements, mass incarceration, mass murder, or a peaceful transfer of political power between different ethnicities. There has never been a case of a peaceful transfer of political power during a demographic shift and demographic shifts occur all the time. Class based systems of representation can avoid poor outcomes by diverting attention away from demographic trends. Class based representation contributes to the deliberation process with role specialization, so the electorate identifies the issues, and then the bicameral process allows the nation to solve their most pressing issues. Economics tensions can be solved with due process. Demographic issues cannot be if the expectations are impossible.

Demographic shifts result when demographic groups previously in the majority try to resist the transition to minority demographic status with minority political power. Class based representation will raise wages, improvement employment outcomes, and fully fund their governments to resolve political instability. If there are better economic outcomes, demographic groups wont over-value the political power associated with majority demographic status. With better outcomes, they will have more trust, and exhibit more patience reducing the probability of conflict. This is why nation building must incorporate econometric and class-based systems of representation into it portfolio of solutions.

The second political union treated in this chapter will be the realignment of Canada, Mexico, and the

United States along the two axes of demographics and econometrics. In this respect, the demographic changes will be more accepted among a greater proportion of the population, with Hispanics already a growing group in the electorate, and Canada contributing to the plurality of an integrated and well-educated population. In terms of economic capability, Mexico represents an opportunity to integrate a large workforce from a developing economy with an emerging market for export to. This might contribute to more integration and cooperation with Central and South America in terms of trade and political maneuvering. Canada is a resource rich country with a strong currency from a more mature economy. They also have significant cultural and political connections with other allies like Australia and the United Kingdom.

Many people think the U.S. made the first effort in forming a more comprehensive union with Mexico and Canada to hedge the growing economic and political power of the European Union. These processes can take decades and generations as is evidenced by the pace in economic and political reform in Europe. The premise was set up immediately after the World War II, and although it has progressed to a free travel zone, a Eurozone, and limited political control over Central Banking and regulation, it is still in a formative phase fully dependent on the support of the individual members. NAFTA could be the first attempt at forming a North American Union between the United States, Mexico, and Canada. This is an important process as it can be repeated, over and over again, in South America, Africa, and Asia.

In the 1980's, Mexico had a population of 69.3 million[92] and a GDP of 194.4 billion[93]. By 2015 Mexico

---

[92] "Mexico Population", Worldbank.org, accessed on July 14, 2017.

had a population of 127 million[94] and a GDP of 1.144 trillion[95]. This represents nearly a 183% increase in population and a 588% increase in GDP. These figures can be used to estimate the total change in representation if it were included in a political union with the United States and Canada.

Canada is possibly our most important trading partner. In the 1980's Canada had 24.6 million citizens[96]a nd $273.85 billion in GDP[97]. By 2015 Canada had 35.9[98] million citizens and $1.551 trillion in GDP[99]. This represents a 146% growth in population and a 566% growth in GDP. The population growth in Canada is nearly equal to that of the United States with a slightly lower GDP growth rate.

To reiterate the statistics from the last simulation, the United States had a population of 227.25 million citizens[100] in the 1980's and a GDP of $2863 billion[101]. By 2015 the population had grown to 321.4 million persons[102] with a 141% increase in total citizenship while

---

http://data.worldbank.org/indicator/ SP.POP.TOTL?locations=MX

[93] "Mexico GDP", Worldbank.org, accessed on July 14, 2017.
http://data.worldbank.org/indicator/NY. GDP.MKTP.CD?locations=MX

[94] "Mexico Population", Worldbank.org, accessed on July 14, 2017.
http://data.worldbank.org/indicator/ SP.POP.TOTL?locations=M

[95] "Mexico GDP", Worldbank.org, accessed on July 14, 2017.
http://data.worldbank.org/indicator/NY. GDP.MKTP.CD?locations=MX

[96] "Canadian Population", Worldbank.org, accessed on July 15, 2017.
http://data.worldbank.org/ indicator/SP.POP.TOTL?locations=CA

[97] "Canadian GDP", Worldbank.org, accessed on July 15, 2017.
http://data.worldbank.org/indicator/NY.GDP.MKTP.CD?locations=CA

[98] "Canadian Population", Worldbank.org, accessed on July 15, 2017.
http://data.worldbank.org/ indicator/SP.POP.TOTL?locations=CA

[99] Canadian GDP", Worldbank.org, accessed on July 15, 2017.
http://data.worldbank.org/indicator/NY.GDP.MKTP.CD?locations=CA

[100] "United States Population", Worldbank.org, accessed on July 14, 2017.
http://data.worldbank.org/indicator/ SP.POP.TOTL?locations=US

[101] "United States GDP", Worldbank.org, accessed on July 14, 2017.
http://data.worldbank.org/indicator/NY. GDP.MKTP.CD?locations=US

the United States GDP had grown to $17.947T[103] with a 626% increase in value.

The combined total population of the United States would grow to 484.3 million which is nearly the entire population of the EU at 509 million[104]. The new GDP of the North American Union would be $20.642T compared to the European Unions $16.23T[105]. There are shared benefits for all parties. The US population may retain majority power, but Canada will gain political influence over its biggest trading partner for exports. Mexico will gain access to federalist tax dollars to battle the mafia and make infrastructure improvements. Mexico will also gain access to more investment dollars from US market while US employers gain access to lower cost labor with equivalent regulatory structure. The United States gains a much smaller border to the rest of the Continent and a larger population to draw on for enlistment during times of emergency.

If the political union was formed in the 1980's, Mexico would command almost 22% of the demographic based representation, with Canada managing just 8%, and the US maintaining majority political power with 70% of the electorate[106]. Compare this to 2015, where Mexico would climb to nearly 26% of the electorate, Canada would shrink to just 7%, and the United States would continue to hold majority party status with 66% of the

---

[102] "United States Population", Worldbank.org, accessed on July 14, 2017.
http://data.worldbank.org/indicator/ SP.POP.TOTL?locations=US

[103] "United States GDP", Worldbank.org, accessed on July 14, 2017.
http://data.worldbank.org/indicator/NY. GDP.MKTP.CD?locations=US

[104] "EU Population", Worldbank.org, accessed on July 15, 2017.
http://data.worldbank.org/indicator/ SP.POP.TOTL?locations=EU

[105] "EU GDP", Worldbank.org, accessed on July 15, 2017.
http://data.worldbank.org/indicator/ NY.GDP.MKTP.CD?locations=EU

[106] Comparison of demographic data and GDP data for U.S., Canada, and Mexico from http://data.worldbank.org/

demographic based representation[107]. Most of the population growth occurred in Mexico but populations tend to stabilize once they acquire mature market status[108], like the US and Canada, so the projections could change after labor standards are improved and Mexican law enforcement receiving substantial increases in funding.

The econometric representation within the NAU presents a different trajectory. In the 1980's, Mexico would capture nearly 6% of the total econometric representation. Canada would claim 8% while the United States would monopolize the chamber with close to 86% of the total GDP based vote. In 2015, Mexico's total proportion would remain at just 5%, while Canada's share would shrink to 7.5%[109]. The United States would retain almost 87% of the total econometric representation in the NAU.

The representational ratios earned by Canada are much lower than most of the states within the Union. In 1980, the Canadians would suffer under a 10:1 ratio in representation. This would grow to 12:1 ratio in representation by 2015. These are in line with the moderate population states in the United States Senate. For instance, Washington has a 7.17 million resident population with a representational ratio of 12 in the U.S. Senate[110]. Missouri also has a representational ratio of 10 with 6 million residents[111].

---

[107] Comparison of demographic data and GDP data for U.S., Canada, and Mexico from http://data.worldbank.org/

[108] "Mature Economy", Thefreedictionary.com, Accessed on July 15,2017. http://financial-dictionary.thefreedictionary.com/Mature+economy

[109] Comparison of GDP data for U.S., Canada, and Mexico from http://data.worldbank.org/

[110] "Factfinder", census.gov, accessed on July 15th, 2017. https://factfinder.census.gov/faces/tableservices/jsf/pages/productview.xhtml?src=bkm k

[111] "Factfinder", census.gov, accessed on July 15th, 2017.

The representational ratios for Mexico slightly higher but far from the most extreme ratios in the Union. In 1980, the Mexicans would suffer under a 15:1 ratio in representation[112]. This would grow to 16:1 ratio in representation by 2015[113]. These are in line with the moderate population states in the United States Senate. For instance, New Jersey has an 8.96 million resident population with a representational ratio of 15 in the U.S. Senate[114]. Michigan also has a representational ratio of 16.9 with 9.92 million residents[115]. This is a compromise that most states make. Mexico should assent to GDP based representation referencing the precedents set by Missouri and Maryland and accept a moderate deficiency in representation like a huge majority of contemporary states.

Representational ratios of 12:1 and 16:1 is far better than the ratios bore by the biggest and largest states in the United States. California has a ratio of approximately 67:1, Texas has a ratio of nearly 47:1, Florida has a ratio of almost 35:1, with New York suffering under a ratio just slightly under 34:1[116]. The median representational ratio is between Louisiana at 7.969 and Kentucky at 7.54[117]. Both Canada and Mexico

---

https://factfinder.census.gov/faces/tableservices/jsf/pages/productview.xhtml?src=bkm
k

[112] Comparison of demographic data for U.S., Canada, and Mexico from
http://data.worldbank.org/

[113] Comparison of demographic data for U.S., Canada, and Mexico from
http://data.worldbank.org/

[114] "Factfinder", census.gov, accessed on July 15th, 2017.
https://factfinder.census.gov/faces/tableservices/jsf/pages/productview.xhtml?src=bkm
k

[115] "Factfinder", census.gov, accessed on July 15th, 2017.
https://factfinder.census.gov/faces/tableservices/jsf/pages/productview.xhtml?src=bkm
k

[116] "Factfinder", census.gov, accessed on July 15th, 2017.
https://factfinder.census.gov/faces/tableservices/jsf/pages/productview.xhtml?src=bkm
k

would be in the above median group indicating a slight deficiency but when they are broken into smaller states, there will be some high higher per capita ratio of GDP than others, although the aggregate representation afforded to the group will remain constant.

Canada would own an 8% margin in both chambers. This was stable over the entire 35-year period. Mexico experienced a 4% gain in the demographic chamber but see no improvement in the econometric chamber. The United States will continue to maintain a majority in both the demographic and econometric chambers of representation. The fears of loss of sovereignty through a political union with Mexico and Canada is not founded on reason or evidence. This is especially true when GDP is used as the representational coefficient for the second chamber.

Over another 70-year period, the United States might be challenged by an 8% increase in Mexican performance and an 8% loss in their own performance, but the spoiler will then be Canada which without coincidence represents a nearly 8% share of the demographic representation[118]. If the trajectory of Mexican population growth starts to conform to other mature economies, the demographic majority enjoyed by the United States and Canada will hold over several more generations. More stability in the demographic representation will result in more support for the N.A.U. in the United States and Canada.

The next most likely change in Union participation will be the United Kingdom with a

---

[117] "Factfinder", census.gov, accessed on July 15th, 2017.
https://factfinder.census.gov/faces/tableservices/jsf/pages/productview.xhtml?src=bkmk

[118] Comparison of GDP data for U.S., Canada, and Mexico from
http://data.worldbank.org/

movement away from the E.U. and towards its historic partners Canada and Australia. The Union can be modeled through the twin axes of demographics and econometrics. There are few sectarian rifts in the populations, and it could easily be expected to be one of the premier political unions in the world.

Australia had 14.7m citizens in 1980 and 23.8m citizens in in 2015[119]. Canada had 24.6m citizens in 1980 and almost 35.9m citizens in 2015[120]. The United Kingdom had 56.3 million persons in 1980 and 65.1m in 2015[121]. The total proportion of population for Australia in 1980 was 15.4%, for Canada it was 25.7%, and for the United Kingdom it was 58.9%[122]. The proportions changed to 19.1% for Australia in 2015, 28.8% for Canada, and 52.2% for the United Kingdom[123].

In the 1980's Australia had 149.66B in GDP and $1.340T in 2015[124]. Canada had $273.85B in GDP in the 1980's and that grew to $1.551T GDP in 2015[125]. The United Kingdom had $564.9B GDP in 1980 and $2.849T GDP in 2015[126]. The proportion of GDP representation in 1980 set Australia at 15.1%, Canada at 27.7%, and the

---

[119] "Australian Population", Worldbank.org, accessed on July 15, 2017. http://data.worldbank.org/ indicator/SP.POP.TOTL?locations=AU

[120] "Canadian Population", Worldbank.org, accessed on July 15, 2017. http://data.worldbank.org/ indicator/SP.POP.TOTL?locations=CA

[121] "UK Population", Worldbank.org, accessed on July 15, 2017. http://data.worldbank.org/ indicator/SP.POP.TOTL?locations=EU

[122] Comparison of population data for Australia, Canada, United Kingdom from http://data.worldbank.org/

[123] Comparison of population data for Australia, Canada, United Kingdom from http://data.worldbank.org/

[124] "Australian GDP", Worldbank.org, accessed on July 15, 2017. http://data.worldbank.org /indicator/NY.GDP.MKTP.CD?locations=AU

[125] "Canadian GDP", Worldbank.org, accessed on July 15, 2017. http://data.worldbank.org/indicator/NY.GDP.MKTP.CD?locations=CA

[126] "UK GDP", Worldbank.org, accessed on July 15, 2017. http://data.worldbank.org /indicator/NY.GDP.MKTP.CD?locations=GB

U.K. at 57%[127]. This changed in 2015 when Australia was allocated 23.3% of GDP, Canada maintained 27%, and the U.K.'s share shrank to just 49.6% of GDP[128].

The largest representational gains were made by Australia with an 8.2% improvement in proportional GDP and a 3.7% gain in proportional Population[129]. Canada also increased their proportion of population by 3%. The biggest representational losses were 7.5% in proportional GDP by the U.K. and a 6.7% loss in proportional population[130]. Canada had a near nominal loss in GDP.

The representational ratios for the GDP representation are minimal with the ratio between 1980's Australia and U.K. being just 3.77 and then shrinking to 2.12 in 2015[131]. The ratio for Canada in the 1980's was 2.06 with it decreasing to just 1.83 in 2015[132]. These are much more moderate than the extremes found in the United States. Australia managed a ratio closer to New Mexico at 3.55 with and Maine at 2.26 when compared to California at 66.8[133]. Canada is best compared to Maine and Rhode Island at 1.80[134]. This demonstrates the GDP

---

[127] Comparison of GDP data for Australia, Canada, United Kingdom from http://data.worldbank.org/

[128] Comparison of GDP data for Australia, Canada, United Kingdom from http://data.worldbank.org/

[129] Comparison of GDP data for U.K., Canada, and Australia from http://data.worldbank.org/

[130] Comparison of GDP data for U.K., Canada, and Australia from http://data.worldbank.org/

[131] Comparison of GDP data for U.K., Canada, and Australia from http://data.worldbank.org/

[132] Comparison of GDP data for U.K., Canada, and Australia from http://data.worldbank.org/

[133] "Factfinder", census.gov, accessed on July 15th, 2017. https://factfinder.census.gov/faces/tableservices/jsf/pages/productview.xhtml?src=bkm k

[134] "Factfinder", census.gov, accessed on July 15th, 2017. https://factfinder.census.gov/faces/tableservices/jsf/pages/productview.xhtml?src=bkm

ratio between the smaller and larger states are much closer with more parity in representation. This power sharing between similar cultures should result in stronger bonds between the nations.

This would be the most natural movement for the three Crown countries seeing that the European Union is moving towards political union and that the United States has a static state of political union. There is safety in numbers and a 120m person economic bloc is far more capable than a 60m person bloc. The new United Kingdom would have access to all three of the biggest markets in the world. It would have Australia in Asia, Canada in North America, and the U.K. in Europe. A perfect situation for industry that can remove most barrios to transport between the allied countries.

The United States would likely forgo a union with Mexico if it could instead forma new economic and political block with the U.K., Canada, and Australia. The total GDP would be equal to $23.687T^{135}$. This is far larger than the E.U. and might gain parity with the GDP growth expected in China over the next 20 years. The total population would be $446.2m^{136}$ which will be just shy of the European Union's population of $509m^{137}$. It will also expand the U.K. and U.S. reach into the Pacific with trading possible through both Australia. It would also provide access the Artic region near the North Pole which could be an important source for natural resources and trade route when the ice melts.

---

k

[135] Summation of GDP data for U.S., Canada, Australia, and U.K. from http://data.worldbank.org/

[136] Summation of population data for U.S., Canada, Australia, and U.K. from http://data.worldbank.org/

[137] "EU Population", Worldbank.org, accessed on July 15, 2017. http://data.worldbank.org/indicator/ SP.POP.TOTL?locations=EU

The total proportion of population in the 1980's was Australia with just 4.6%, Canada with 7.6%, the U.K. with 17.4%, and the U.S. with 70.3%[138]. The proportions changed slightly by 2015 with Australia gaining 5.3% of total demographic representation, Canada acquiring 8.0%, the U.K. shrinking to 14.5%, and the U.S. growing to 72.0%[139]. Demographic shifts shouldn't disrupt politics to any great degree with most positions holding steady and where cultural integration and shared identity is already present. If anything, the growth in Hispanic populations will be checked by the expansion of the Anglo populations in the U.K., Australia and Canada, but their inclusion will open relations with the developing countries in Central and South America. Diversity is a huge advantage when demographic concerns are mitigated with the use of an econometric chamber based on GDP.

The total proportion of GDP in the 1980's was 3.9% for Australia, 7.1% for Canada, 14.7% for the U.K., and 74.3% for the U.S.[140]. By 2015, Australia grew to 5.65%, Canada shrank to 6.5%, the UK decreased to 12.0%, and the U.S. increased to 75.8%[141]. The changes in GDP reflected similar changes in population. This arc might be altered by the flow of federal tax subsidies and investment dollars after the union is formed. The unrestricted trade zones will also benefit those partners losing ground in the GDP based chamber. The promise of

---

[138] Comparison of population data for U.S., U.K., Canada, and Australia from http://data.worldbank.org/

[139] Comparison of population data for U.S., U.K., Canada, and Australia from http://data.worldbank.org/

[140] Comparison of GDP data for U.S., U.K., Canada, and Australia from http://data.worldbank.org/

[141] Comparison of GDP data for U.S., U.K., Canada, and Australia from http://data.worldbank.org/

econometric representation is one that accommodates these short-term trends by allowing the participants to adjust and change the expected outcome. Despite interim losses, the act of unionization may substantially change the current trajectory, and this uncertainty should be enough incentive to strike an agreement. The biggest representational gains were found in Australia with a 1.8% gain in proportional GDP and the United States with a 1.43% gain in proportional GDP[142]. The United States also earned a 1.6% gain in demographic representation over the 35-year period[143].

The biggest representational losses were in the U.K. with a 2.6% loss in GDP and a 2.9% loss in population[144]. All other values remain stable over the 35-year period. Despite the gains and losses in representation, the partners would be far better off with the political union than if they remained independent of the E.U. and U.S. Military cooperation is a huge component of any political union, and access to new territories will benefit all. If the partners accept the higher ratio of defense spending found in the United States, with greater parity in technological capacity, the inclusion of another 120m persons[145] will improve the West's ability to counteract an activist China attempting to export its despotism to the world. It is the implied threat that will discourage misbehavior and facilitate stronger trade between the spheres.

---

[142] Comparison of GDP data for U.S., U.K., Canada, and Australia from http://data.worldbank.org/

[143] Comparison of Population data for U.S., U.K., Canada, and Australia from http://data.worldbank.org/

[144] Comparison of GDP data for U.S., U.K., Canada, and Australia from http://data.worldbank.org/

[145] Summation of GDP data for U.K., Canada, and Australia from http://data.worldbank.org/

Looking at the unthinkable is also justified. For the next simulation, the United States will separate into two independents and competing blocs. This section doesn't advocate for a split, but it certainly entertains its possibility citing the debt default threats and numerous government shutdowns during a period of demographic shifts and unprecedented wealth inequality. Hints of secession have precedent. Not only was one war over secession already fought in the U.S. with the culture still frequently referenced but the U.K. recently voted to leave the E.U.[146]. Scotland has reciprocated threatening an exit from the U.K. There are parts of Spain currently entertaining secession and years ago Quebec threatened to leave Canada. It isn't farfetched to suggest a split between urban states and rural states in context of the growing political divide and economic disparity between regions.

A dissolution could be peaceful after a debt default or violent after a compromised Presidential election. Any permanent split in the union would be a less-than-optimal outcome. There is a strength in numbers and if the United States can preserve its territorial boundaries while improving the quality of its democratic entitlement, it will be far better off than any other outcome. Any outcome other than preserving the union would result in a catastrophic loss in GDP and violent change in the electorate. These simulations are Gedanken experiments, motivated only by the access of demographic and economic data in the U.S. with the convenience of declared political sympathies.

Dividing the nation between urban states and rural states is a theoretical exercise. This book uses heuristics

---

[146] "EU Referendum results", bbc.com, accessed on KJuly 16, 2017.
http://www.bbc.com/news/politics/eu_referendum/results

and assumes that the more urban states are on the coasts and the more rural states are in the southern and central regions. To be clear, there are some sparsely states included within the urban group and some densely populated states included within the rural group. These boundaries are hardly fixed and static with political affiliation changing over time and subject to electoral outcomes that won't be considered in this treatment of the subject. Often, the affiliation is due to proximity to other states that share these geo-spatial properties.

These simulations fix the coastal states (urban) to California, Colorado, Connecticut, Delaware, Hawaii, Illinois, Maine, Maryland, Massachusetts, Michigan, Minnesota, Nevada, New Hampshire, New Jersey, New Mexico, New York, Oregon, Pennsylvania, Rhode Island, Vermont, Wisconsin, and Washington. Washington D.C. is added to the GDP and population for the urban states although it is not a state. The central and southern states (rural) are fixed to Alabama, Alaska, Arizona, Arkansas, Florida, Georgia, Idaho, Indiana, Iowa, Kansas, Kentucky, Louisiana, Mississippi, Montana, Missouri, Nebraska, North Carolina, North Dakota, Ohio, Oklahoma, South Carolina, South Dakota, Tennessee, Texas, Utah, Virginia, West Virginia, and Wyoming. This isn't an arbitrary assignment, although it is not substantiated by any specific history.

For convenience, the coastal states are considered one independent bloc of nations with the central and southern states relegated to a competing bloc. If the rural states seceded from the union, they would have 161m persons in 2015[147] with a little more than 8.00T in GDP

---

[147] "Factfinder", census.gov, accessed on July 16th, 2017.
https://factfinder.census.gov/faces/tableservices/jsf/pages/productview.xhtml?src=bkm
k

in 2015[148]. This is contrasted to the urban states having 160m persons[149] in 2015 with 9.83T GDP in 2015[150]. They would have nearly equal populations, but the urban states would have almost 122% advantage in GDP[151]. This has profound effects on demographics and econometrics of the new nation. This is more evident when examining the prospects of an economic union with the other allied nations or proximate nations.

The first union examined will be the central and southern states and Mexico. This looks like an unorthodox or unlikely combination but if war can provoke future union formation, then this simulation is warranted. It should be noted that Hispanic populations are growing within the border states, including Texas and Florida, and they will have a dominant role in any democratic society and political system in the newly incorporated states. Although the current proportions aren't accurate for an immediate incorporation, the trends may hold true for the incorporation of the union after a period of occupation. By occupying Mexico, a 1933-mile border[152] can be transformed into an approximate 400-mile border[153] which has obvious implications for a population that sets border control as a high priority.

---

[148] "Tools (interactive data, regional data, GDP in current dollars, by year)", bea.gov, accessed on July 16, 2017. Reports run for each year, only "Red States" from page 42.

[149] "Factfinder", census.gov, accessed on July 16th, 2017. https://factfinder.census.gov/faces/tableservices/jsf/pages/productview.xhtml?src=bkm k

[150] "Tools (interactive data, regional data, GDP in current dollars, by year)", bea.gov, accessed on July 16, 2017. Reports run for each year, only "Red States" from page 42.

[151] Comparison of 2015 GDP for Red Stats and Blue States

[152] Janice Beaver, "U.S. International Borders: Brief facts", CRS Report for Congress, accessed on September 19.2017. https://fas.org/sgp/crs/misc/RS21729.pdf

[153] Randal Archibald, "In Trek North, First Lure is Mexico's Other Line", New York Times, last modified April 26, 2013. http://www.nytimes.com/ 2013/04/27 /world/americas/central-americans-pour-into-mexico-bound-for-us.html

In 2000, the central and southern states had a population of 136 million[154] and a GDP of 4.44T[155] while Mexico had only 98.9m persons[156] and a 683.6B economy[157]. This shifted to nearly 161m persons[158] in the US by 2015 with 7.99T GDP[159]. Mexico acquired 127m persons[160] in 2015 with 1.144T GDP[161]. The total population of this new nation would be 288m persons[162] which is nearly 89% that of the current 321m[163] person population of the United States[164]. The total economic output is 9.143T[165] falling short of the standalone GDP of the coastal states as well as the current GDP of China. Mexico does help them make up ground in terms of population and GDP, but they must consider other options to achieve parity with their competitors.

---

[154] "Factfinder", census.gov, accessed on July 18th, 2017.
https://factfinder.census.gov/faces/tableservices/jsf/pages/productview.xhtml?src=bkm
k
[155] "Tools (interactive data, regional data, GDP in current dollars, by year)", bea.gov, accessed on July 16, 2017. Reports run for each year, only "Red States" from page 42.
[156] "Mexico Population", Worldbank.org, accessed on July 18, 2017.
http://data.worldbank.org/indicator/ SP.POP.TOTL?locations=MX
[157] "Mexico GDP", Worldbank.org, accessed on July 18, 2017.
http://data.worldbank.org/indicator/NY. GDP.MKTP.CD?locations=MX
[158] "Factfinder", census.gov, accessed on July 18th, 2017.
https://factfinder.census.gov/faces/tableservices/jsf/pages/productview.xhtml?src=bkm
k
[159] "Tools (interactive data, regional data, GDP in current dollars, by year)", bea.gov, accessed on July 16, 2017. Reports run for each year, only "Red States" from page 42.
[160] "Mexico Population", Worldbank.org, accessed on July 18, 2017.
http://data.worldbank.org/indicator/ SP.POP.TOTL?locations=MX
[161] "Mexico GDP", Worldbank.org, accessed on July 18, 2017.
http://data.worldbank.org/indicator/NY. GDP.MKTP.CD?locations=MX
[162] Summation of Mexico and Red States' population 2015 estimates.
[163] "Factfinder", census.gov, accessed on July 18th, 2017.
https://factfinder.census.gov/faces/tableservices/jsf/pages/productview.xhtml?src=bkm
k
[164] Summation of Mexico and Red States' GDP 2015 estimates
[165] "Mexico GDP", Worldbank.org, accessed on July 18, 2017.
http://data.worldbank.org/indicator/NY. GDP.MKTP.CD?locations=MX

Mexico lost nearly 13% of its total proportion of GDP[166] compared to the U.S.[167] based representation over the period of 2000-2015 while gaining nearly 10% in demographic representation[168]. This is still a net loss of nearly 3% over the 15-year period. This may be enough incentive for the central and southern states to seek out the union. If the trends continue, the central and southern states will capture more of the electorate and have a developing economy to resource for labor efficiencies and maximize exports to other markets. The Mexicans will capture federal tax subsidies and investment dollars at a high ratio due to the disparity in currency values. Mexico will gain nearly 44% of the entire demographic based chamber by 2015 which will be incentive to agree to the terms[169].

The central and southern states might only have a 55% majority in the demographic chamber[170] but the ratio grows to nearly 87% in the GDP based chamber[171]. They can effectively dictate the terms of reform and economic management through a bicameral process with emphasis on free market tendencies or outcomes. This current trend demonstrates an increase in the disparity in GDP favoring the central and southern states despite the faster economic growth in Mexico. The Mexicans may only have 13% proportion of representation in the econometric chamber[172]

---

[166] "Mexico Population", Worldbank.org, accessed on July 18, 2017.
http://data.worldbank.org/indicator/ SP.POP.TOTL?locations=MX

[167] "Tools (interactive data, regional data, GDP in current dollars, by year)", bea.gov, accessed on July 16, 2017. Reports run for each year, only "Red States" from page 42.

[168] Comparison of 2015 populations in Mexico and the Central and Southern States.

[169] Comparison of previously cited 2015 populations in Mexico and the Red States found on page 42

[170] Comparison of previously cited 2015 populations in Mexico and the Red States found on page 42

[171] Comparison of previously cited 2015 GDP for Mexico and the Red States on page 42

but they will contribute nearly 44% to Presidential elections[173]. Through the dichotomy between demographic representation and econometric representation, power can be effectively shared between developing economies and mature economies.

In 30 years, Hispanic populations may have significant majorities in Texas, Florida, Nevada, New Mexico, Arizona, and other states. Incorporating Mexico into a union may make more sense to a larger proportion of the population of that period. This simulation is predicated on the central and southern states maintaining high quality democratic entitlements after secession, which is not necessarily guaranteed. However, simulations of non-democratic nations are out of bounds of this book. If the central and southern states form an imperial democracy and incorporate Mexico, they may seek to expand their border to Cuba as well.

Cuba represents a mistake made by the American established decades ago. New administrations might want to correct those passed errors. Support for this agenda will be found in Florida and the larger voting Cuban population. Cuba has a nominal economy and won't disrupt the proportion of representation apportioned through GDP, but it does have a viable population of nearly 12 million making it one of the larger states in the hypothetical Union[174].

Cuba would capture nearly 4% of the total popular vote in the new nation according to 2015[175]

---

[172] Comparison of previously cited 2015 GDP between Mexico and the Red states on page 42

[173] Comparison of previously cited 2015 population between Mexico and the Red States found on page 42

[174] "Cuban Population", worldbank.org, accessed on July 18, 2017. http://data.worldbank.org/indicator /SP.POP.TOTL?locations=CU

[175] Comparison of Mexico, Cuba, and U.S. 2015 populations

populations. Mexico would drop to just 42%[176] and the central and southern would drop to nearly 54%[177]. GDP representation would be almost unchanged by the inclusion of Cuba's paltry 77B economy[178]. However, due to the proportional method of representation, Cuba would gain exactly 1 representative. This would be an over-representation of the state, but most contemporary democracies have equivalent examples to justify the relationship. With 87% of the GDP based representation still in central and southern states' possession[179] they won't feel threatened by the expansion of the electorate to include Mexico and Cuba. The central and southern state will seek to acquire an equivalent level of power and prestige to the station they previously held while part of the United States. This will require them to incorporate states they wouldn't otherwise pursue.

The coastal states are slightly more formidable than the southern and central States. The coastal States have approximately the same population at 160m[180] but they capture slightly more than 60% of GDP with $9.85T GDP in 2015[181]. If the coastal states joined in union with Mexico and Canada, it would regain almost 100% of the lost population from the former United States[182]. The new nation would have 323m persons[183] with approximately

---

[176] Comparison of Mexico, Cuba, and U.S. 2015 populations

[177] Comparison of Mexico, Cuba, and U.S. 2015 populations

[178] "Cuban GDP", worldbank.org, accessed on July 18, 2017.
http://data.worldbank.org/ indicator/NY.GDP.MKTP.CD?locations=CU

[179] Comparison of Mexico, Cuba, and U.S. by GDP

[180] "Factfinder", census.gov, accessed on August 9th, 2017.
https://factfinder.census.gov/faces/tableservices/jsf/pages/productview.xhtml?src=bkm
k

[181] "Tools (interactive data, regional data, GDP in current dollars, by year)", bea.gov, accessed on August 9th, 2017.

[182] "Factfinder", census.gov, accessed on August 9th, 2017.
https://factfinder.census.gov/faces/tableservices/jsf/pages/productview.xhtml?src=bkm
k

70% of the former economy at \$12.5T GDP[184]. It is far from the \$18T[185] economy they used to manage, but the United American States (UAS) would still be able to accomplish many of the goals and tasks it previously favored. There is strength in numbers and the coastal will seek out permanent alliance with its neighbors to mitigate the counter-productive relationship it has with the Red States.

The coastal states will seek to incorporate the Canadians for two major reasons. First, they represent a mature economy with a diverse and educated electorate. Secondly, the represent a free movement zone and will connect the states on one coast with the states on the other coast. Mexico represents a developing economy for the investment dollars of the coastal states. In this respect, the central and southern states occupied a similar position being the recipient of most federal tax subsidies. Mexico may also bring with it improved relations to Central and South America. A multi-cultural and multi-lingual UAS should improve trade between the three regions.

From 2000-2015, Mexico's proportion of demographic representation would grow from 36% to 39% of the total union[186], Canada would remain stable at just 11%[187], and the coastal states will fall from 53%[188] to just 50%[189]. A 4% improvement for Mexico is their

---

[183] Accessed on 8.9.2017 and retrieved from US Census data and World Bank data

[184] "U.S. GDP", Worldbank.org, accessed on 8.9.2017.
http://data.worldbank.org/indicator/NY.GDP.MKTP.CD?locations=US&view=chart

[185] \$12.5T/\$18T "U.S. GDP", Worldbank.org, accessed on 8.9.2017.
http://data.worldbank.org/indicator/NY.GDP.MKTP.CD?locations=US&view=chart

[186] "U.S. GDP", Worldbank.org, accessed on 8.9.2017.
http://data.worldbank.org/indicator/NY.GDP.MKTP.CD?locations=US&view=chart

[187] Derivative of demographic data from US Census and World Bank

[188] Derivative of demographic data from US Census and World Bank

[189] Derivative of demographic data from US Census and World Bank

incentive to join the Union[190]. However, during the same period, Mexico will stabilize at only 9% of the econometric representation[191], while the Canadians grow from 10% to 12%[192], and the coastal states fall from 80% to 78%[193]. The coastal states will continue to maintain a huge majority in the GDP based chamber providing incentive to form the Union.

The coastal states have more homogenous populations than the central and southern states and aren't in crisis over recent demographic shifts. This will keep them open to political union with its neighbors. Mexico offers a bridge into Central America and South America. It also represents a growing market for exports and investment. The coastal states have other options available to them. The UK recently voted to exit the EU and may be an opportunity for Union with the coastal states, Canada, and Australia.

A union between Canada, Australia, England (UK), and the former United States would have 284m citizens[194] with nearly $15.6T GDP[195]. It might have lost 50m persons[196] but it would limit its GDP loss to just 14% of GDP[197]. The United States (dropping America from the title) would have to adopt a 2nd generation government to increase efficiency, and this can be accomplished by either eliminating the Filibuster and Presidential Veto or by adopting a Parliamentarian structure. The nations already have extremely tight

---

[190] Derivative of demographic data from US Census and World Bank

[191] Derivative of BEA data and World Bank data

[192] Derivative of BEA data and World Bank data

[193] Derivative of BEA data and World Bank data

[194] Derivative of World Bank data and US Census data

[195] Derivative of World Bank data and BEA Data

[196] Derivative of World Bank data and US Census data

[197] Derivative of World Bank data and BEA Data

military relationships, and their citizens have similar ideas about healthcare, education, and civil liberties. They could integrate quickly and easily. It would be a formidable association that would be nearly equivalent to the EU in GDP[198] post Britain exit, with territory in both Europe and Asia.

From 2000-2015, Australia would gain nearly 1% in demographic representation[199], the United Kingdom would see a loss of just 1%[200], Canada would lose only 0.5%[201]. and the coastal states would lose almost 1%[202]. These are stable trajectories over 15 years. It is assumed they can be sustained indefinitely. The former United States retains most of political power, but the Crown Countries capture almost 44% giving them plenty of opportunities to negotiate with the individual parties in the coastal states[203]. Most political markets are very competitive with alternating administrations and each region would be effectively split between multiple political parties. It is doubtful nationalist attitudes would divide the nation by region rather than party.

The econometric chamber demonstrates other trends. Over the period of 2000-2015, Australia increased from 5% to nearly 9%[204], the UK saw zero growth maintaining 18%[205], while Canada's representation grew from 9% to nearly 10%[206]. The coastal states saw their

---

[198] "EU GDP", Worldbank.org, accessed on August 9, 2017.
http://data.worldbank.org/indicator/NY.GDP.MKTP.CD?locations=EU&view=chart

[199] Derivative of World Bank data and US Census Data

[200] Derivative of World Bank data and US Census data

[201] Derivative of World Bank data and US Census data

[202] Derivative of World Bank data and US Census data

[203] Derivative of World Bank data and US Census data

[204] Derivative of World Bank data and BEA data

[205] Derivative of World Bank data and BEA data

[206] Derivative of World Bank data and BEA data

majority shrink from 68% to just 63%[207]. However, the coastal states would still have clear majorities in both chambers. Their citizens will be open to trade up on representation formerly apportioned to the central and southern being allocated to Canada, Australia, and the UK. Despite the loss in GDP and population, the new United States might be a more viable and capable nation.
'

Great Britain might be able to retain the support and cooperation of Scotland[208] and Northern Ireland[209], both of which are concerned over the split with the EU, if it considered a political union with the US. Otherwise, it could fracture amidst the calls for secession circulating in the world. The UK would be the hub for all European exports from its allies, helping to replace its former status as EU financial capital. The UK has a long history of alliance with the United States, and this might influence Canada and Australia to make similar decision.

The last simulations will be central and southern states with Mexico and Canada. It is assumed that many of the citizens in the central and southern states will actively seek to offset the demographic changes caused by integrating Mexico with the populations found in Canada. Mexico, Canada, and the central and southern states combined to form nearly 324m persons[210] and

---

[207] Stephen Castle, "Scotland Votes to Demand a Post "Brexit" Independence Referendum", Nytimes.com, last modified March 28, 2017.
https://www.nytimes.com/2017/03/28/world/europe/scotland-britain-brexit-european-union.html?_r=0

[208] , "What does brexit mean for northern ireland", Newstatesman.com, last modified June 24, 2016. https://www.newstatesman.com/politics/uk/2016/06/what-does-brexit-mean-northern-ireland

[209] , "What does brexit mean for northern ireland", Newstatesman.com, last modified June 24, 2016. https://www.newstatesman.com/politics/uk/2016/06/what-does-brexit-mean-northern-ireland

[210] Derivative of World Bank and US Census data

$10.69T GDP[211]. This is almost equivalent to the current GDP of China[212] and with a large portion of the economy remaining developing with a faster GDP growth rate, the Central States of America (CSA) could make some gains on the emergent economic superpower.

One concern is the precipitous drop in federal revenues after the loss of the coastal. Despite the coastal states paying 57% of taxes[213] they only receive 50% of the federal tax subsidies[214]. One of the reasons for this discrepancy is base location in the country and the huge disparity in enlistment. Most of the military bases are in the central and southern states with a huge nearly 2:1 advantage in enlistment for those states[215]. The central and southern states won't be able to support the military they control and the loss of federalist tax support.

The 20% difference in federalist tax subsidies will contribute to massive public finance deficits for the central and southern states after secession or dissolution of the union[216]. In some cases, the loss of Blue state subsidies could represent a loss of economic stimulus by a margin of nearly 2-3% of GDP. In the same respect, New Jersey and Connecticut would almost double the amount of money they receive back from the economic union once the dependency of the central and southern

---

[211] Derivative of World Bank and US Census

[212] "Chinese GDP", Worldbank.org, accessed on August 9, 2017.
http://data.worldbank.org/indicator/NY.GDP.MKTP.CD?locations=CN&view=chart

[213] "Tools (interactive data, regional data, GDP in current dollars, by year)", bea.gov, accessed on July 16, 2017. Reports run for each year, "Red state GDP" compared to "Blue State GDP" in proportion, found on page 42.

[214] "2015 Data Book, state revenue data", irs.gov, accessed July 2nd 2017.
https://www.irs.gov/pub/irs-soi/15databk.pdf

[215] "Military Active-Duty Personnel, Civilians by State", governing.com, accessed on August 9, 2017. http://www.governing.com/gov-data/military-civilian-active-duty-employee-workforce-numbers-by-state.html

[216] Derivative of BEA data and IRS data – comparing differences in state revenues with contributions made.

states is ended. On average, New Jersey and Connecticut only receive back 60% of the contributions they make to the federal government[217]. The repatriation of $60B in federal spending represents nearly 10% of annual GDP to New Jersey[218].

The central and southern states' tentative grasp on democracy in the region could suffer an immediate insult to their economies and public finance systems. However, if the central and southern states did pursue union formation it could produce a more equitable and stable outcome. A union with a population of 324m[219] with a GDP close to 11T[220] would continue to be a potent force in the world, especially if it remains democratic. The United States is one of the largest oil producing nations in the world and these resources are concentrated in the central and southern states. This is a double-edged knife. It could be a hugely lucrative outcome for residents helping offset the initial loss of federal tax subsidy, but it could also invite instability. The newly incorporated states might succumb to the allure and curse of oil production and metamorphosis into a state resembling the OPEC nations or those like Russia, Venezuela, or Nigeria.

If these deficiencies can be overcome, the combined benefits of increased military prowess and massive oil production could make the republic an incredibly successful ally and trading partner. Mexico, Canada, and the central and southern states combined to form nearly 324m persons[221] and 10.69T GDP[222]. This is

---

[217] "2015 Data Book, State Revenue Data", irs.gov, accessed August 9th 2017. https://www.irs.gov/pub/irs-soi/15databk.pdf

[218] "2015 Data Book, State Revenue Data", irs.gov, accessed August 9th 2017. https://www.irs.gov/pub/irs-soi/15databk.pdf

[219] Derivative of World Bank data and US Census data

[220] Derivative of World Bank data and BEA data

almost equivalent to the current GDP of China and with a large portion of the economy remaining developing with a faster GDP growth rate, the Confederated States of America (CSA) could make some gains on the emergent economic superpower.

For instance, Mexico would fall to just 37% of the entire electorate in 2000, with the central and southern states retaining 51% of representation, and Canada capturing almost 12%[223], Canada represents another mature economy with ideologies that reflect strong democratic institutions. Mexico is also strongly rooted in democracy, but it is suffering under terrible corruption and crime at the moment. By 2015, Mexico will represent only 39%, with the central and southern states falling to 49%, and Canada declining to 11%[224]. The central and southern states will need to form coalitions to lead the union, which will be complicated by internal demographics, and external relationships with both Mexico and Canada.

GDP based representation provides an opportunity for the central and southern states to maintain a clear representational advantage despite the majority in the cumulative electorate diminishing. In 2000, Mexico will have nearly 12% of the GDP representation, while Canada has 13%, and the central and southern states maintain 75%[225]. The former United States will have a clear majority to lead from. This is reinforced over the 15-year period, with Mexico falling to 11%, Canada growing to 15%, and the central and southern states

---

[221] Derivative of World Bank data and US Census data

[222] Derivative of World Bank data and BEA data

[223] Derivative of World Bank data and US Census data

[224] Derivative of World Bank data and US Census data

[225] Derivative of World Bank data and BEA data

declining slightly to 74% in 2015[226]. This large majority in representation should be incentive enough for the central and southern states to entertain the union, especially if they are attempting to recover after a split with the coastal who controlled nearly 60% of the GDP of the former United States[227].

The central and southern states don't have to fear losing representation in the demographic chamber if they retain their influence in the econometric chamber. Politics is complicated, and the central and southern states will already have some of the most complicated demographics in the world. They will have a large and growing Hispanic population in the Border states and Florida, with a large and stable African American population in the South. They will need to navigate the political environment as a minority demographic group anyway, so the inclusion of Mexico and Canada don't do much to alter their current or expected future state.

The point of these simulations is not to predict likely outcomes. It is to suggest how economic representation could provide more opportunities for union formation or nation building. The peaceful integration of states is a far more effective method for expanding free trade and improving civil liberties and voting rights. However, war is a feature of our geo-political environment and the rise in wealth inequality and expected disruptions from climate change will accelerate the rate of conflict. The world has benefited from an unnatural state of peace for the last 70 years. This period might be over with the contraction in the European

---

[226] Derivative of World Bank data and BEA data

[227] "Tools (interactive data, regional data, GDP in current dollars, by year)", bea.gov, accessed on July 16, 2017. Reports run for each year, "Red state GDP" compared to "Blue State GDP" in proportion, found on page 42.

Union, the loss of authority and power in the United States, and the rise of a despotic China as economic and military superpower. Nation building will be an important component for foreign policy in the near future and econometric representation may offer unique benefits.

Bibliography:

"2015 Population Tables", Census.gov, accessed on July 3rd,
    2017.https://www.census.gov/data/tables/2016/demo/popest/nat
    ion-total.html
"Afghanistan GDP", Worldbank.org, accessed on July 14,
    2017. http://data.worldbank.org/indicator/NY.
    GDP.MKTP.CD? locations=AF
"Afghanistan Population", Worldbank.org, accessed on July
    14, 2017. http://data.worldbank.org/indicator/-SP.POP.TOTL?
    locations=AF
Archibald, Randal. "In Trek North, First Lure is Mexico's
    Other Line", New York Times, last modified April 26, 2013.
    http://www.nytimes.com/ 2013/04/27/world/-americas/central-
    americans-pour-into-mexico-bound-for
    -us.html
"Australian Population", Worldbank.org, accessed on July 15,
    2017. http://data.worldbank.org/ indicator/SP.POP.TOTL
    ?locations=AU
"Australian GDP", Worldbank.org, accessed on July 15, 2017.
    http://data.worldbank.org/indicator/NY.GDP.MKTP.CD
    ?locations=AU
"Battlefield Vietnam", PBS.org, accessed on June 24th, 2017.
    http://www.pbs.org/battlefieldvietnam/
Beaver, Janice. "U.S. International Borders: Brief facts", CRS
    Report for Congress, accessed on September 19/2017.
    https://fas.org/ sgp/crs/misc/RS21729.pdf
Boland, Stephanie. "What does Brexit mean for northern
    ireland", Newstatesman.com, last modified June 24, 2016.
    https://www.newstatesman.com/politics/uk/2016/-06/what-
    does-brexit-mean-northern-ireland
"California Community Facts", Census.gov, accessed on July
    1st, 2017.https://factfinder.census.gov/faces/nav/jsf/-
    pages /index.xhtml
"California GDP", worldbank.org, accessed on July 1st, 2017.
    http://data.worldbank.org/indicator/NY.GDP.MKTP.CD?locati
    ons=CA
"California Population Totals", worldbank.org, accessed on

July 1st, 2017. http://data.worldbank.org/indicator/-
SP.POP.TOTL?locations=CA

"Canadian GDP", Worldbank.org, accessed on July 15, 2017.
http://data.worldbank.org/indicator/NY.GDP.MKTP.CD
?locations=CA

"Canadian Population", Worldbank.org, accessed on July 15,
2017. http://data.worldbank.org/ indicator/SP.POP.-
TOTL? locations=CA

Castle, Stephen. "Scotland Votes to Demand a Post "Brexit"
Independence Referendum", Nytimes.com, last modified March
28, 2017. https://www.nytimes.com/2017/03/28/
world/europe/scotland-britain-brexit-european-union.html?_r=0

"Chinese GDP", Worldbank.org, accessed on August 9, 2017.
http://data.worldbank.org/indicator/NY.GDP.MKTP.CD
?locations=CN&view=chart

"Cuban GDP", worldbank.org, accessed on July 18, 2017.
http://data.worldbank.org/indicator/NY.GDP.MKTP.CD?
locations=CU

"Cuban Population", worldbank.org, accessed on July 18,
2017. http://data.worldbank.org/indicator /SP.POP.-
TOTL ?locations=CU

Donnely, T. and Rosen,J. "Political polarization killed the
filibuster", Theatlantic.com. Last modified 4/8/2018.
https://www.theatlantic.com/politics/archive/2017/04/
political-polarization-killed-the-filibuster/522360/

"EU GDP", Worldbank.org, accessed on July 15, 2017.
http://data.worldbank.org/indicator/NY.GDP.MKTP.CD
?locations=EU

"EU Population", Worldbank.org, accessed on July 15, 2017.
http://data.worldbank.org/indicator/ SP.POP.TOTL?
locations=EU

"EU Referendum results", bbc.com, accessed on KJuly 16,
2017.http://www.bbc.com/news/politics/eu_referendum/-results
"European Wars and Battles", Thoughtco.com, accessed on
7/10/2017. https://www.thoughtco.com-/european-wars-and-
battles-4133312

"Factfinder", census.gov, accessed on July 18th, 2017.
https://factfinder.census.gov/faces/tableservices/jsf/pages/produ
ctview.xhtml?src=bkmk

"Finance: Afghanistan", World Atlas, accessed on April 2nd,
2018 at https://www.worldatlas.com/finance/afghanistan/

gdp.html

"Florida Community Facts", Census.gov, accessed on July 1st, 2017.https://factfinder.census.gov/faces/nav/jsf/pages/index.xhtml

Florida, Richard. "Is life better in americas red states", Nytimes.com, last modified 01/3/2015. https://www-.nytimes.com/2015/01/04/ opinion/sunday/ is-life-better-in-americas-red-states.html

Frank, Aaron. "Could automation lead to chronic unemployment? Andrew Macafee sounds the alarm", forbes.com, last modified 7/19/2012. https://www.fo-rbes.com/sites/singularity/ 2012/07/19/could-auto-mation-lead-to-chronic-unemployment-and-rew-mcafee-sounds-the-alarm/#60603fda1a31

"GDP per capita India", StatisticsTimes.com, accessed on April 2nd, 2018 at http://statisticstimes.com/economy/-gdp-capita-of-india.php

"Genocides, Politicides, and Other Mass Murder since 1945", Genocidewatch.net, accessed on 7/12/2017. http://-genocidewatch.net/genocide-2/genocide-and-politicide/

Gruber, John. *Public finance and public policy*. New York, NY: Worth Publishers, 2015.

Hampson, Rick. "Afghanistan Americas Longest War", CBS, Last modified on May 31, 2010. http://abcnews.go.com/ Politics / afghanistan-americas-longest-war/story?id= 10770029

Halloran, Richard. "The Sad, Dark End of the British Empire", Politico.com, last modified on August 26, 2014. http://www.politico.com/magazine/story/2014/08/the-sad-end-of-the-british-empire-110362

"Indian states by GDP", Worldatlas.com, accessed on 2nd, 2018 at https://www.worldatlas.com/articles/indian-states-by-gdp.html

"Iraq GDP", Worldbank.org, accessed on July 14, 2017. http://data.worldbank.org/indicator/NY.GDP. MKTP.CD ?locations=IQ"Iraq: GDP per capita", Trading Economics, accessed on April 2nd, 2018 from https://tradingeconomics.com/iraq/gdp-per-capita

"Iraq Population", Worldbank.org, accessed on July 14, 2017. http://data.worldbank.org/indicator/ SP.POP.TOTL ?locations=IQ

Khasraw, Zana. "Who is responsible for Iraq's sectarian
        violence", last modified June 7, 2013. https://www.open-
        democracy.net/zana-khasraw-gul/who-is-responsible-for-
        iraq%e2%80%99s-sectarian-violence
Mankiw, Gregory N. *The Essentials of Economics* (6th ed.).
        Stanford: CT Cengage Learning, 2015.
"Mature Economy", Thefreedictionary.com, Accessed on July
        15,2017. http://financialdictionary.thefreedictionary.com/
        Mature+ economy
"Mexico GDP", worldbank.org, accessed on July 1st, 2017.
        http://data.worldbank.org/indicator/NY.GDP.MKTP.CD
        ?locations=MX
"Mexico Population Totals", worldbank.org, accessed on July
        1st,2017.http://data.worldbank.org/indicator/SP.POP.TO
        TL?locations=MX
"Military Active-Duty Personnel, Civilians by State",
        governing.com, accessed on August 9, 2017.
        http://www.governing.com/gov-data/military-civilian- active-
        duty-employee-workforce-numbers-by-state.html
Mishel, L., Gould,E., and Bivens, J. "Wage stagnation in
        nine charts", www.edpi.org, last modified 1/6/2015.
        http://www.epi.org/publication/charting-wage-stagnation/
Monaghan, Angela "Wealth inequality top 01 worth as much
        as bottom 90", Theguardian.com, last modified
        11/13/2014.https://www.theguardian.com
        /business/2014/nov/13/us-wealth-inequality-top-01-worth-as-
        much-as-the-bottom-90
"News Releases, regional GDP by state", bea.gov, access on
        July 1st, 2017. https://bea.gov/newsreleases/regional-/gdp_state
        by State", bea.gov, accessed on July 1st, 2017. https://be-
        a.gov/newsreleases/regional/gdp_ state/qgsp_newsrele-ase.htm
"Population apportionment", Census.gov, accessed on July 14,
        2017. https://www.census.gov/population/apport-ionment/
        about /computing.html
Przeworski, Adam. Minimalist Conception of Democracy: A
        Defense." In Democracy's Value edited by Shapiro, I. and
        Hacker-Cordon, C. Cambridge: Cambridge University.
Rosenberg, Jennifer. "The Major wars and conflicts of the
        20th century", Thoughtco.com, last modified on
        8/13/2018 https://www.thoughtco.com/major-wars-and-
        conflicts-20th-century-1779967

"State Summaries", USAspending.gov, accessed on July 2nd, 2017. https://www.usaspending.gov/transparency/ Pages/StateSummaries.aspx

"Texas Community Facts", Census.gov, accessed on July 1st 2017.https://factfinder.census.gov/faces/nav/jsf/pages/ index.xhtml

"The economics of violence", economist.com, last modified 4/14/2011http://www.economist.com/node/18558041

"The house explained", house.gov, accessed on July 14, 2017. https://www.house.gov/the-house-explained

"Tools (interactive data, regional data, GDP in current dollars, by year)", bea.gov, accessed on July 16, 2017.

"UK GDP", Worldbank.org, accessed on July 15, 2017. http://data.worldbank.org/indicator/NY.GDP.MKTP.CD ?locations =GB

"UK Population", Worldbank.org, accessed on July 15, 2017. http://data.worldbank.org/indicator/SP.POP.TOTL?locati ons=EU

"United States GDP", worldbank.org, accessed on July 1st, 2017.http://data.worldbank.org/indicator/NY.GDP.MKT P.CD?locations=US&view=chart

"United States Population", Worldbank.org, accessed on July 14, 2017. http://data.worldbank.org/indicator/ SP.POP.TOTL?locations=AF

Weisinger, Jordan (2018). The Fountain: Nation building with econometric representation. South Carolina: Create Space, 2018.

"Wyoming, Community Facts", Census.gov, accessed on July 1st,2017.https://factfinder.census.gov/faces/nav/jsf/pages index.xhtml

Biography

Jordan David Weisinger graduated from the Johns Hopkins University with a M.S. in Data Analytics and Policy (2019), Northwestern University with a M.A. in Public Policy and Administration (2017), and the University of Massachusetts Amherst with a M.B.A in General Management (2015). His undergraduate degree is in Literature from the University of Delaware (2000) where he focused on literature from the Gilded Age in the United States. Jordan has written several books detailing how alternate forms of democracy can be used for nation building,

He focuses on high-quality systems that deliver anti-discriminatory and anti-corruption properties, improving their long-term viability and interest from special interest groups. He has written about GDP-based systems (2017), Income-based systems (2018), Tax-based systems (2018), and Asset-based systems (2020) and intends to continue exploring how econometric systems of representation can improve outcomes for nation building efforts. Recently he has written books focusing on non-violent strategies executives and legislators can use to resist authoritarian movements or successfully wage a war for independence. Strategic Non-violent Institutional Protests are intended to make it more likely that the econometric systems of representation described in earlier books are used for nation building in wars of succession, secession, or democratization.